Managing Behaviour in the Primary School

Managing Behaviour in the Primary School

Jim Docking

David Fulton Publishers

London

Published in association with the Roehampton Institute

David Fulton Publishers Ltd
2 Barbon Close, London WC1N 3JX

First published in Great Britain by
David Fulton Publishers 1990

©Jim Docking

British Library Cataloguing in Publication Data

Docking, J.W. (James Woodrow) *1936–*
  Managing behaviour in the primary school.
  1. Great Britain, Primary schools. Classrooms. Management
  by teachers
  I. Title
  372.110240941

  ISBN 1-85346-141-5

Typeset by Chapterhouse, Formby
Printed and bound in Great Britain by
BPCC Wheaton Ltd. Exeter

Contents

Acknowledgements

During the course of preparing this book, I have received invaluable help from primary school heads and teachers, who have generously given of their time to talk to me about their approaches to managing pupil behaviour and allowed me to make observations in their schools. My special thanks are due to the following, some of whom kindly provided information for accounts of special projects described in the text:

Elizabeth Belilios; Richard Brading (Acting Head) at Hillbrook Primary School, Tooting, London; Norma Bramley (Headteacher), Krystyn Hollaway and Timothy Rome at Normand Park Primary School, Fulham, London; Sr Jo Goggins (Headteacher), Brenda Casey and Chris Earley at St. Anne's RC JMI School, Kennington, London. Margaret Etherington (Headteacher) and Jacquie Goodall at Hillcross Middle School, Morden, Surrey; Liz Saunders.

I am also grateful to Martyn Long, Educational Psychologist for Norfolk County Council, for his personal communication about the scheme described on p.54.

My thanks also to Jacquie and David Coulby and Falmer Press for permission to reproduce (p.82) the 'Page from a Success Book' originally published in *Education and Alienation in the Junior School*, (1990), edited by J. W. Docking.

Lastly, I must thank my wife, Anne, who patiently read through the penultimate draft, provided important corrections, and made many valuable comments.

Jim Docking
July, 1990

Chapter 1

The Elton Inquiry

> In view of public concern about violence and indiscipline in schools and the problems faced by the teaching profession today, to consider what action can be taken by central government, local authorities, voluntary bodies owning schools, governing bodies of schools, headteachers, teachers and parents to secure the orderly atmosphere necessary in schools for effective teaching and learning to take place.
>
> *Terms of Reference to the Elton Inquiry*

Background to the inquiry

In March 1988, the Government set up a committee to undertake an inquiry into school discipline and make recommendations accordingly. The Report, *Discipline in Schools* (DES, 1989), was published twelve months later. The Committee was chaired by Lord Elton, who had not only been a minister in several government departments but had also enjoyed a career as a history teacher in a grammar and comprehensive school and as a lecturer in a college of education. The other six members came from colleges, schools and industry. Unfortunately only one member, the head teacher of a junior school, had employment in primary education. However, the committee received evidence and suggestions from numerous teachers of young children and visited many primary schools.

The Inquiry was set up against a background of reports by the teacher unions which suggested that violent and other serious indiscipline was widespread and growing in both primary and secondary schools. The most widely publicised survey was conducted by the Professional Association of Teachers (PAT) in conjunction with the *Daily Express* which gave the findings front-page treatment. Under the headline 'Scandal of Beaten-Up Teachers', readers were told that:

Teachers are being constantly beaten up by violent pupils .... One in three masters and mistresses questioned in our survey said they had been physically attacked by children. And almost all of them said that indiscipline was on the increase in schools, with 17 out of 20 teachers saying they were facing a rising tide of violence.

Daily Express, 25 November 1987

The evidence produced suggested that serious behaviour problems were by no means confined to secondary schools. One headmistress reported that she had been kicked in the back, punched and verbally abused by children as young as five. In general, the source of the troubles experienced by teachers was seen to lie in factors which were outside the school's immediate control rather than deficiencies in the schools themselves. Parents were blamed for not controlling their children, or teaching them right and wrong; TV was blamed for its constant portrayal of violent behaviour which children then imitated; and the law was blamed for tying teachers' hands by prohibiting the use of corporal punishment.

The General Secretary of PAT subsequently wrote to the Prime Minister, Margaret Thatcher, pointing out that, 'the National Curriculum cannot be delivered if there is national chaos in the classroom'. Urging the Government 'to grapple with the disciplinary crisis which threatens to overwhelm the education system', he insisted that a commission of inquiry be set up as 'a public declaration that the Government acknowledges the existence of a crisis'.

Evidence collected during the mid-1980s by members of other teacher unions and the National Association of Head Teachers, though less sensationally reported, also suggested that there was widespread disruption in schools and that the position was getting worse. The setting up of the Elton Inquiry can therefore be seen as a response to pressure from the teacher unions to demonstrate that the Government was doing something.

In contrast to the teacher union evidence, however, a much more positive picture was emerging in reports by Her Majesty's Inspectorate for Schools (HMI) and professional researchers. First of all, the *scale* of the problem was seen to be much less. According to HMI (1987), 'The overwhelming majority of schools are orderly communities in which there are good standards of behaviour: poor behaviour is unusual, and serious indiscipline a rare occurrence' (para. 10). In the Junior School Project, involving over 2000 pupils in fifty schools in London (Mortimore *et al.* 1988), class teachers reported three-quarters of their children to be 'cooperative', and less than ten per cent 'disobedient'. A comparable finding emerged in Dawson's (1987) Barnsley study, which included twenty-two primary schools, only 1.5 per cent of children being perceived by their teachers as causing 'an unusually high degree of concern'. Similar results to these emerged in non-union studies of secondary schools.

Secondly, the *nature* of the problem was seen to be different in reports by independent investigators. As in the teacher union reports, teachers were found to be subjected daily to stress through pupil behaviour. However, the vast majority of incidents were seen to be matters such as talking and mucking around rather than violence and verbal abuse. Amongst primary schools in the West Midlands, for instance, Wheldall and Merrett (1988) found that the most frequent behaviour problems were 'talking out of turn' (reported by 55 per cent of teachers) and 'hindering other children' (21 per cent); only 1 per cent of teachers identified aggression against staff as a common occurrence. Similarly, Blatchford *et al.* (1987) found negligible evidence of aggression towards teachers in a sample of thirty-three London infant schools.

Thirdly, the non-union surveys were more assertive in attributing a major *source* of behaviour problems to the schools themselves. Although parents and the media were by no means exonerated, and although behaviour problems were generally more manifest in 'difficult' localities, schools in similar catchment areas were found to have markedly different standards of behaviour. This pointed to the fact that some heads and staff were more effective than others in promoting good conduct. For example, behaviour scores in the Junior School Project, mentioned above, differed substantially between the most and least successful schools, and sharp differences remained even after adjustment to take account of a wide range of pupil background factors. Similar conclusions were reached in Stephenson and Smith's (1989) study of bullying. In this, the marked differences in aggression between children from one school to another seemed to be associated with staff attitudes towards the problem. In short, the general picture which emerged from the non-union studies was that the general atmosphere and particular practices of schools and individual teachers can, and does, make a substantial difference to pupil behaviour.

How is it possible to explain the discrepancies between the findings of the teacher unions, on the one hand, and professional researchers and HM Inspectors on the other? Part of the answer lies in methodological flaws in the union surveys. These included the use of self-selecting samples which may not have been representative of teachers in general, response rates to questionnaires as low as 4 per cent, and loaded or vague questions which were of doubtful validity and reliability. The Elton Committee therefore wisely refrained from assuming at the start of their inquiry that discipline problems were increasing or taking the form of a major crisis with which schools were unable to cope. Instead, they commissioned their own research – the largest investigation of its kind which had been carried out in this country – and visited schools, mostly in urban areas, both in this country and abroad.

Findings and observations

A national survey of teachers' perceptions of behaviour problems in schools was undertaken as part of the Elton Inquiry by John Gray and Nicholas Sime of Sheffield University Educational Research Centre. For the primary age-phase, a questionnaire was sent to 1212 teachers in 250 schools throughout England and Wales. In contrast to the very low response rates elicited by the teacher union surveys, returns were received from the vast majority of teachers (89 per cent for primary schools) with little variation between regions. The survey findings could therefore be confidently interpreted as representative of all teachers and schools.

Teachers were first asked to report on different types of problem behaviour which they had encountered during the previous week in the classroom. As in the earlier independent studies, the most troublesome matters cited were not aggression towards staff or verbal abuse, but relatively minor incidents which were damaging in their cumulative rather than individual effects. For example, in primary schools 97 per cent of teachers said that during the previous week they had had to deal with pupils talking out of turn, while 90 per cent reported pupils hindering each other and 85 per cent reported pupils making unnecessary, non-verbal noise. Additionally, 60 per cent or more had had to deal with pupils wandering around the room without permission, 'calculated idleness', and general rowdiness. By contrast, physical aggression towards staff in primary schools was mentioned by only 2.1 per cent, and verbal abuse by only 7 per cent.

However, although physical attacks on staff were rare, 74 per cent of primary teachers said that they had had to deal with aggression between pupils at least once during the previous week in lesson times. Also, when they were asked to report on behaviour in the corridors and playground, 86 per cent mentioned that they had witnessed at least one incident of physical aggression between pupils over the past week, and a large majority had encountered other kinds of inconsiderate pupil-to-pupil behaviour. Again, however, violence towards teachers was rarely reported (1.6 per cent).

When asked to comment on the gravity of behaviour problems, the staff of about one in twenty primary schools described their experiences as 'serious', though the proportion was higher in schools where a large number of pupils were 'below average' or came from areas of social and economic hardship. In two-thirds of the schools the teachers thought that behaviour problems were 'not at all serious' or 'no problem at all'. Four out of ten said they had no pupils in their class who were 'difficult to deal with'; and as few as two out of ten said that there were particular behaviours which they found difficult to cope with.

Overall, the picture that emerged from this investigation was not the one painted by the media or the teacher unions. Certainly there were teachers who had been subjected to aggressive and abusive behaviour from pupils towards them, and some incidents had indeed been serious. However such violence was rare, although pupil-to-pupil aggression was a fairly common occurrence. In the absence of earlier comparative data, the researchers had not asked teachers whether behaviour was worse than it had been in the past. It was clear, however, that the main problem at present was the cumulative stress-inducing effects of frequent, low-level disruption. The importance of these findings is not just that they go some way in setting the record straight but that they give grounds for optimism. The kinds of problem behaviour which teachers most often experience are of the kind which, given appropriate support, can normally be dealt with by improved classroom management and school ethos.

The Elton Committee also visited schools, mainly in urban areas. Their observations confirmed earlier findings from HMI and professional researchers that schools in similar kinds of catchment areas can experience very different levels in standards of behaviour, and that this is largely a reflection of different school policies and teacher strategies:

> When we visited schools we were struck by the differences in their 'feel' or atmosphere. Our conversations with teachers left us convinced that some schools have a more positive atmosphere than others. It was in these positive schools that we tended to see the work and behaviour which impressed us most. We found that we could not explain these different school atmospheres by saying that the pupils came from

different home backgrounds. Almost all the schools we visited were in what many teachers would describe as difficult urban areas. We had to conclude that these differences had something to do with what went on in the schools themselves.

Elton Report p. 88

In trying to explain these school differences, the Committee argued that the schools with the best standards were those which concentrated on trying to encourage good behaviour instead of spending most of their energy in dealing with problem behaviour:

> Our visits showed us that good schools can reduce misbehaviour to an absolute minimum. While some schools seem preoccupied with bad behaviour, others have concerted policies for raising expectations and improving standards. The schools we saw which had such positive policies seemed to be very successful in creating an orderly and purposeful atmosphere. They had marginalised bad behaviour by promoting good behaviour. The central thrust of our recommendations is towards promoting good behaviour among pupils.

Elton Report, p. 66

Of course, as the Committee pointed out, there are limits to what individual teachers can do in isolation, for much depends on the leadership given by the head, the concerted efforts of the staff as a whole, and the relationships which the school develops with parents.

Recommendations for action

In addition to the visits to schools, the Committee's deliberations were informed by oral evidence from representatives of many organisations and government departments, including each of the teacher unions, HM Inspectors, and the National Children's Bureau. Interviews were also held with a number of researchers who had investigated problem behaviour in schools. Written evidence was received from local education authorities, teacher-training establishments and many other organisations and individuals.

Aided by this wealth of advice, the Committee made 138 recommendations. Many of these concern parents, LEAs, police, teacher-trainers, curriculum councils, voluntary bodies, government and other bodies outside the school. Here we are concerned with the main recommendations which related to the responsibilities of individual teachers and schools, particularly as they affect the primary sector. It should be borne in mind, however, as the Committee rightly recognised, that just as the success of each class teacher depends on the concerted efforts of the school community, so does the success of each school depend upon support from local and central government.

The matters for which the Committee considered that schools themselves should take responsibiltity can be grouped under six headings:

(1) *Classroom management skills*

The central recommendation was that more schools would be orderly places if teachers could be helped to become more effective managers of group behaviour: 'Group management skills are probably the single most important factor in achieving good standards of classroom behaviour' (p. 70). It was a mistake, the Committee argued, for teachers to assume that such skills were simply a gift, for this meant that failure to keep class control was often unwarrantably attributed to personal inadequacy, which in turn generated teacher stress. Because the Committee recognised that teachers could *learn* class management skills, it recommended that all initial teacher-training courses must include at least ten hours of practical training specifically in managing groups of pupils.

(2) *Mutual staff support*

Behaviour problems were seen to be stress-inducing partly because of the tradition whereby teachers were expected to cope alone. Seeking help, the committee said, should not be taken as an admission of professional incompetence. Teachers could help each other, and the children, if they learned how to give each other constructive support. The committtee therefore recommended that there should be increased provision for school-based staff development, with timetables of those who had just joined the profession reduced by half a day each week to allow opportunities for in-service, for observing other teachers, and for visiting other schools. Heads were seen as playing a pivotol role in providing a context in which the skills of individual teachers could be most effectively employed.

(3) *School ethos*

A large number of recommendations were concerned with ways in which schools could develop more positive atmospheres by promoting a sense of community. Heads and senior staff were seen as the main agencies in ensuring that their schools develop consistent codes of conduct based on a high degree of consensus among teachers, pupils and parents. It was suggested that strategies here should include measures to recognise and praise good behaviour as well as finding effective ways of dealing with unwanted behaviour. As regards the latter, punishments should help pupils to distinguish between minor and serious misdemeanours. They should be applied with fairness and consistency, and therefore not be humiliating or administered to whole groups of children.

The Committee noted how behaviour problems sometimes arose as a result of stereotyping particular groups of pupils as troublemakers, and recommended that teachers be sensitive to this danger and its injustice. Academically less-able boys and boys of Afro-Caribbean extraction were seen as particularly vulnerable.

Heads and teachers together were urged to be alert to signs of bullying and racial harassment, dealing firmly with such behaviour. It was thought very important for victims to feel able to talk to staff about aggressiveness experienced from other children and receive protection and support.

Schools were also asked to develop policies for dealing with the physical appearance of the buildings: this would include not only measures to reduce litter, graffiti and damage to property, but also to help children value each other's achievements through the effective display of their work.

(4) *Involving parents*

The Committee recognised that good discipline often went hand in hand with policies to develop positive relations with parents. The strategies recommended here included keeping parents informed, providing a welcoming atmosphere and easy access to staff, involving parents in the classroom and home learning schemes, and telling them about their children's good (as well as unacceptable) behaviour. It was regarded as vital to involve parents at an early stage in the development of behaviour problems rather than as a last resort – not least because children's behaviour at home often differed from that in school.

(5) *Involving pupils*

Equally the Committee urged schools to create opportunities for involving the pupils themselves in managing the school community, finding out their views about behavioural matters and encouraging their active participation in shaping and reviewing the school's behaviour policy. It was also thought to be important for staff to provide scope for more pupils to feel significant in school by having their non-academic achievements recognised and for them to be given the opportunity to take on appropriate responsibilities.

(6) *The role of governors*

Governors were given a separate section in the Report since, under the Education Act 1986, heads are required to comply with any written statement on behaviour issued by the governing body.

The Committee recognised the role of school governors to be important in two main respects. One was in developing the school's discipline policy. In their school guidelines, governors were recommended not only to incorporate the principles of good practice contained in the Elton Report but also to help in monitoring and evaluating standards of behaviour, to require heads to supply regular reports on school discipline, and to include this topic as an item in their annual report to parents.

The other major concern of governors as regards school behaviour was in appointing staff. The need was to employ teachers whose relationships with pupils would be based on mutual respect and who could work well in a team. Heads in turn needed to be good team leaders, able to combine purposeful leadership with a consultative management style.

The Government's response

In paying tribute to the work of the Elton Committee, the then-Education Secretary, Kenneth Baker, announced to Parliament on 13 March 1989 that the Government was taking action to follow up the Committee's recommendations. Amongst the measures was the requirement that practical training in managing pupil behaviour would be a required part of initial teacher training, and that national standards would be laid down to ensure that the teacher-trainers themselves spent specified amounts of time in the classroom to ensure they had sufficient recent practical experience. These recommendations were subsequently embodied in a set of criteria, published in the DES Circular 24/89, for the approval of initial teacher-training courses.

In addition, the Government announced that management training programmes for headteachers and senior staff would emphasise the skills required to motivate and lead staff and to manage institutional change. The Goverment would also give the management of pupil behaviour national priority in the Local Education Authority in-service training grants (£1.7m was eventually allocated for 1990–91), and Education Support grants would be made available to help LEAs tackle the problems of truancy and pupils presenting particular behaviour difficulties.

Chapter 2

Managing Behaviour – What Does It Mean?

> I have accepted the committee's recommendation that in future all initial teacher-training courses should include separate, compulsory elements of practical training in how to manage pupil behaviour.
> *Announcement to Parliament by the Secretary of State for Education, 13.3.89.*

Like many other areas of work, teaching is riddled with its special jargon. Furthermore, the jargon is constantly changing. In curricular matters, children are given physical 'education' rather than, as formerly, physical 'training'; they complete pieces of 'creative writing' instead of 'compositions'; they study 'technology' instead of 'craft'; under the National Curriculum they are subjected to a series of 'assessment tasks', not 'tests' or 'examinations'; and those who experience difficulty with the curriculum are no longer 'backward' but have 'special educational needs'. The jargon is also changing in matters to do with social behaviour. Traditionally, teachers have talked about 'controlling *children*' by subjecting them to 'discipline'. Whilst these terms continue to enjoy general usage and still have a legitimate role to play, the phrase 'managing *behaviour*' seems to be gaining currency.

Although new educational terminology sometimes amounts to little more than new labels for old practices, it often represents a shift of emphasis and change in approach. This is certainly the case with the curriculm examples cited above, and it seems true also with respect to the term 'managing pupil behaviour'. The argument of this chapter is that this expression is now often used because many teachers want to distance themselves from the restricted assumptions, aims and practices which are often implied in traditional talk about 'controlling children' and 'exercising discipline'. The word 'control' has mechanistic connotations, implying that teachers order their charges around without respecting their personhood. There is little room for discourse, listening to and trying to understand the voice of the pupil. The word 'discipline' in one sense is importantly associated with 'disciple', suggesting that teachers and pupils should be working together towards an idealised kind of behaviour. However, more often it is associated with 'disciplinarian' and notions of inflexible, even harsh, external control. A shift to the use of the expression 'managing pupil behaviour', then, reflects a growing desire amongst teachers to re-examine traditional policies and practices, as reflected in such notions as 'controlling pupils', and to develop more positive approaches.

The next step in this chapter is, therefore, to examine the respects in which some of the popular conceptions, or models, of behaviour problems are found wanting, and to outline the kind of model which is finding more favour in schools. This is followed by an overview of some implications of the new model for managing pupil behaviour, and succeeding chapters consider some of the practical consequences for professonal practice in primary schools.

Assumptions about the nature of behaviour problems

The attributional language of staffroom discussion often reveals a good deal about the assumptions teachers hold about the causes and nature of pupil behaviour which threatens classroom order. We sometimes hear of 'problem pupils' and those who are 'naughty', 'disruptive', 'disturbed', 'devious', 'troublemakers', 'disaffected' . . . and so on. Other teachers, however, prefer to avoid dwelling upon assumptions about the children's character or mental condition. They talk more in terms of individuals' 'problem behaviour' and its effects rather than of 'problem pupils' and their psychological make-up.

These different ways of speaking convey contrasting beliefs about the most productive way of thinking about discipline problems in school and the kind of response which we should make to the problems. Staffroom reactions to the expression we use can also serve to encourage or discourage the degree to which we maintain our perception of the problem. If, for example, we refer to a pupil as a 'troublemaker', we are stating our belief that the child is being deliberately difficult, and we are probably also trying to persuade other teachers to think likewise. Were another teacher to say, 'Oh, I don't know, I think he (or she) is more troublesome than a troublemaker', this could persuade us to think again and reconceptualise the problem as one which has unpleasant consequences for everyone concerned (including the child in question) but not as one which is necessarily due to the pupil's bad motives. However, if instead everyone nods, smiles, raises their eyes to heaven or makes a comment like 'Yes, I know, he's a real devil with me too', we are reinforced in our belief that the child is simply setting out to make trouble and our classroom relationships will be coloured accordingly.

Of course, sometimes we use one term rather than another because it is in vogue or because we have simply 'picked up' the term and fallen unthinkingly into the habit of using it. However, expressions which become part of our everyday vocabulary gradually come to influence and shape our perceptions of the problem under discussion. So that the more we describe a child as, say, a 'troublemaker', the more that child in our mind takes on the characteristics of a troublemaker. We then no longer see 'the child' so much as 'the troublemaker'.

It appears, then, that the staffroom vocabulary of pupil behaviour, of which 'troublemaker' is an example, represents different popular models of the causes and nature of problem behaviour and what our response to it should be. Teachers vary in the extent to which they subscribe to one model or another, but here we shall identify four which, although not mutually exclusive, represent broad attributional tendencies amongst some members of the profession. A growing number of teachers, however, are rejecting all four models as representing an unwarrantably limited understanding of behaviour problems in school, and failing to generate constructive approaches to the management of pupil behaviour.

We begin, then, with the *'troublemaker' (or 'naughty pupil') model*. This not only characterises problem behaviour as intentionally and even malevolently produced, but makes the assumption that the child can control it. The term 'disruptive pupil' (rather than disrupting), perhaps makes similar assumptions. Even the Elton Committee, in spite of its generally positive recommendations, makes unfortunate use of the term 'bad behaviour' throughout its report. Although this is certainly preferable to talking about 'bad pupils', the regular use of an expression which has such strong moral overtones conveys the suggestion, unwittingly, that it is pupils' 'badness' which lies at the root of most discipline problems.

The use of expressions such as 'troublemaker' and 'naughty pupil' probably serves as a defensive mechanism. For by attributing behaviour problems to the child's intentions and bad motives, teachers exempt themselves from blame whilst also conveying the message that any change in their own attitude is conditional upon the child taking the first step.

This was demonstrated in a study of 4- to 11-year-olds who presented problems in the classroom. Rohrkemper and Brophy (1983) analysed teachers' reactions to various types of learning and behaviour problems, including aggression and defiance, shyness, rejection by peers, hyperactivity, short attention span, and social immaturity. The findings showed that the more the child's problem posed a threat to the teacher's classroom control, the more the teacher took the view that the child was intentionally creating the problem and that it was up to the child to control it. Thus, teachers were prepared to develop special programmes and put themselves out for children who were rejected by their peers, who were less able (as distinct from underachieving) and who were shy or socially immature; but they tended to blame, reprimand and punish those who were aggressive, disobedient or underachieving.

teachers response

Of course, if we are to regard young children as persons, then we must also attribute to them intentionality and blameworthiness. To deny children intentionality would be to deny them the very characteristic that makes them human and capable of 'responsible' behaviour. Some children on some occasions, even in infant classes, do seem to be deliberately 'naughty' and 'out to make trouble', just as some children on some occasions seem to go out of their way to be kind and considerate. Nonetheless intentionality does not exist in a vacuum. Without denying that problem behaviour is often intentional and sometimes malevolent, we still need to explain how it is that some pupils seem bent on 'making trouble'. Moreover, a tendency to see pupils with behaviour problems in terms of pupils with bad intentions leads to a style of response which does little to ameliorate the problem. The teacher's classroom management becomes characterised by perpetual nagging, criticising, scolding, reprimanding and sometimes punishing. Certainly children sometimes do deserve to be reprimanded and punished, but if they experience these measures as typical management strategies they come to resent the imputation of 'being bad', and this helps to maintain the problem.

The *'problem pupil' model* of behaviour difficulties encapsulates yet another set of popular perceptions. Here it is some kind of illness which is taken to be the source of the problem behaviour: there is something 'wrong' with the child. This medical model has important consequences for the teacher's responsibility. Children are said to suffer from 'disorders' and therefore to be in need of 'treatment', which only 'experts' can give; and because the teacher lacks the necessary expertise, the child must be 'referred' to someone else with the requisite professional skills. This may involve sending the child to a special unit or special school. It is not suggested here that the notion of a disordered personality has no scientific basis or that referrals are invariably inapproapriate, but simply that thinking of problem behaviour in terms of 'problem pupils' can have unproductive consequences for the management of behaviour in school generally. For although one consequence (in stark contrast to the effects of 'troublemakers' imputations) has been the development of more humane and caring attitudes, and although children have undoubtedly often been helped by the treatment received, the result of perceiving problem behaviour in this way is to deny the skill of teachers and parents, encouraging them to believe that they are powerless to effect a change in the behaviour themselves, even with support.

Thirdly, there is the *'problem home' model*. In a recent investigation by Croll and Moses (1985), 428 junior school heads and teachers were asked about their perceptions of pupils who were experiencing behavioural problems. In many cases the cause was attributed to 'within child' factors such as the pupils' intentions or temperament, but the dominant explanation, representing two out of every three cases, was in terms of deficiencies in the children's home circumstances, including the way their parents brought them up. By contrast, in only 3.8 per cent of cases did teachers acknowledge that the child's conduct could be attributed to arrangements in school or classroom management styles. The Elton Committee found a similar reaction among teachers giving reasons for their discipline problems, the majority citing family instability, conflict, poverty and parental indifference or hostility to school.

It thus seems that teachers frequently blame factors outside the school for behaviour problems that occur within it. A consequence of this perception of problem behaviour has been, in some cases, to deter individual teachers and schools from paying sufficient attention to the contribution which they are making to maintaining, and even generating, the problem behaviour. For whereas in the 'troublemaker' and 'problem pupil' models it is the child or the 'expert' who has to accept the main responsibility for changing the problem behaviour, in the 'problem home' model it is the parent. Undeniably, some children's problem behaviour in school is, at least in part, a consequence of adverse home circumstances. Yet it is misleading to assume that they are the only explanations or even the main ones, for, as we can all testify from everyday experience, the way individuals behave is affected by the context in which they are placed. We may feel more cooperative if the weather is sunny, or if we are in the company of people we like or admire, or even if we are in a certain room or building. Behaviour in school is therefore materially affected by a range of school factors as well as home factors, including the teachers' expectations of the child's behaviour and their response to the behaviour, the teachers' classroom management and teaching styles, and the general ethos of the school.

While factors which are outside the immediate control of teachers may predispose a child to behave disruptively in school, the extent to which that child realises such a tendency depends upon the quality of life experienced at school. For instance, children who come from homes where there is a high level of stress due to disharmony may or may not use the school to vent frustration, depending on how they believe they are valued and have status in the school community. As studies such as the Junior School Project (Mortimore *et al.*, 1988) and others cited in the last chapter have shown, heads and teachers can and do promote good behaviour even in schools with 'difficult' intakes.

Fourthly, and more recently, the *'disaffected pupil' model* has come into vogue. This certainly has the advantage of turning attention away from 'within child' and 'within home' factors and focussing on features of the school environment which are within teachers' control. Yet this too represents an unwarrantably restricted perspective. As Jacquie and David Coulby (1990) have put it, describing children in school as 'disaffected' suggests that they are little red soldiers expressing righteous indignation about unsatisfactory features of our society, such as racism, classism and sexism, which are reflected in relationships in school; or, more simply, it suggests resentment at being treated with disrespect by the teachers. This is not in any sense to deny that children sometimes have good reason to feel resentment, a point which was emphasised in the previous paragraph. However, conceptualising problem behaviour mainly in terms of disrespectful teachers, who are then made the scapegoat for all problem behaviour, is as misleading and unhelpful as always blaming the children or their parents. The term 'alienation' is now sometimes used instead of 'disaffection'. As the Coulbys point out, this can be useful as long as it encourages teachers to focus their attention on matters from which pupils feel alienated, but not if it encourages a reversion to assumptions about mental illness by setting up the category of 'alienated pupil'.

Each of these four 'popular' models, as reflected in the everyday attributional language of problem behaviour, fails to do justice to the range of factors that could be affecting pupil behaviour and too easily lays the blame – and therefore the responsibility for change – at one door rather than another. Children's behaviour is the product of a number of interacting factors, the relative importance of each varying from one child to another.

Fortunately, more and more teachers are subscribing to a model which recognises the multifaceted nature of behaviour problems in school. This is sometimes called a *systems model*. Here, pupils are seen as functioning within a network of inter-related systems such as the family, the peer group, the classroom, the playground and the school at large. Each system is made up of interacting elements, or aspects of the situation, which influence, and are often influenced by, the child's behaviour. Thus in the classroom, the elements clearly include the pupils and the teacher, but they also incorporate the curriculum, the resources, the grouping system, the rules, furniture layout and so on – all affecting the child's behaviour and often being affected by it. The playground can also be regarded as a system whose elements not only comprise the pupils who also make up the child's classroom system but also younger and older children from other classes. In addition there are the playground supervisors, the space available, facilities for play, and playground customs, rules and sanctions. In the school at large the elements comprise all the pupils, all the staff and the head, plus the school rules and expectations, the procedures for assembly, the length of lessons and playtimes, the layout of the buildings, specialist facilities, and so on, where again influences work in all directions. The family, neighbourhood and peer group systems contain further sets of elements operating in this interactive way.

In the systems model, therefore, the child's behaviour is seen as a function of numerous interacting elements in various overlapping systems. It follows that bringing about any significant change in behaviour involves changing the nature of the key elements that make up the various systems in which the child operates. The consequences of this model for the school's response to problem behaviour are that intervention is taken at a number of levels to take account of the range of elements that affect the child's behaviour in school. Adherence to the systems model does not therefore entail the belief that all the responsibility for change in pupils' behaviour must lie with just one party, whether it is the pupils, parents, teachers, support services or 'society', before the behaviour can improve. All parties are responsible. However, since the problem behaviour occurs in the school, the *initiative* needs to be taken by teachers, and it is elements within the school system and its sub-systems (classroom, corridors, playground) which will receive the most attention. In the rest of this chapter, we consider the variety of initiatives that many primary schools are now taking and which effectively reflect the systems model.

The scope of behaviour management

As we have seen, managing pupil behaviour according to the systems approach involves more than 'controlling pupils' in the conventional sense because the initiatives taken must do justice to the *range* of elements in the various systems that affect the child's behaviour in school. Initiatives will certainly include classroom processes, but will also involve policies and practices in the school at large, including those that affect relationships in the playground and travel to and from school. Family and peer group influences will also be taken into account. The number of possible elements which might be included in any review of behaviour policy is therefore vast, but the main ones centre round three broad groupings. These are: developing pro-active rather than reactive policies and strategies; improving pupils' behaviour towards each other; and enlisting the active participation of the parents, the pupils and the whole staff.

Pro-active policies and strategies

The first initiative involves a determination to stand back, in collaboration with colleagues, and examine pedagogic and classroom management styles. The inclusion of 'pedagogic' as well as 'management' styles here is important since the two are inter-related. There is a strong overlap between factors that contribute to effective pupil learning and factors that contribute to acceptable pupil behaviour. To suggest, as the Elton Report did (on page 57), that 'good behaviour makes effective teaching and learning possible' is to relate only half the story since (as Elton effectively acknowledges in subsequent passages) effective teaching also makes good behaviour possible!

Traditional notions of 'controlling pupils' and 'exercising discipline' have tended to involve the idea that teachers who are successful in achieving orderly behaviour are those whose management styles essentially consist of keeping a tight reign on their classes by reprimanding and punishing as children step out of line. In recent years this notion has been challenged by evidence from classroom observation studies. Much of the research work originates in the United States, but the ideas are gaining currency in this country and were clearly recognised by the Elton Committee.

Successful class management is now seen to depend upon three complementary strategies which are pro-active rather than re-active: those which pre-empt problem behaviour, those which promote and reinforce good behaviour, and those which encourage pupils to think positively about their learning potential, competencies and personal worth.

(1) *Pre-empting problem behaviour*

The importance of the teacher's skill in pre-empting problem behaviour owes much to the work of Jacob Kounin of Wayne State University. The problem which he investigated concerned a fact which we all know: that pupils behave better with some teachers than with others. By analysing videotapes of many lessons in elementary schools, Kounin (1970) soon found that the more successful teachers were not necessarily those who were most ready to reprimand and punish culprits or who relied on 'crisis management' strategies to deal with misbehaviour once it had occurred: they were those who anticipated behaviour problems by taking measures to prevent them arising in the first place. Following from this work, various researchers in the U.S.A. and Great Britain have confirmed Kounin's findings, and have identified a number of key group management skills which make all the difference to the quality of classroom behaviour. We shall examine these in the next chapter.

(2) *Promoting and reinforcing good behaviour*

Another major challenge to the idea that orderly class behaviour is essentially a function of efficient reactive strategies comes from behavioural psychology. According to the Law of Effect, an action is more likely to be repeated if the perpetrator finds it a rewarding experience. In the classroom, attention-seeking behaviour will often unwittingly be reinforced because such behaviour has pay-off for the pupils concerned – i.e. they get the recognition they are seeking from the teacher and the other children, even if this is negative attention.

Wise teachers, however, seize on the *good* behaviour of children, and ensure that *this* is reinforced through praise or reward. A system of strategies has thus been developed which are encapsulated in the phrase 'catch the child being good'.

Not surprisingly, the Elton Committee found that schools with the better-behaved pupils were those which concentrated on promoting desired behaviour rather than stamping out unwanted behaviour, for the achievement of the first made the second less necessary. The main features of this positive approach to classroom behaviour are discussed in Chapter 4. Of course, teachers who emphasise the promotion of good behaviour will still need to deal with incidents of undesirable behaviour: but the manner of their reprimanding and their use of punishment will be more constructive. In short, their approach to correcting children's behaviour is also positive. This is the subject of Chapter 5.

(3) *Promoting positive pupil self-evaluations and expectations of success* self esteem

In recent years a wealth of research evidence has demonstrated the impact of teachers' verbal and non-verbal language on children's evaluations of themselves – their sense of self-worth, their motivation to learn, and their beliefs about their capabalities. By what they say and don't say, and what they do and don't do, teachers set up positive or negative expectations for achievement, they enhance or deflate pupils' self-esteem, and they influence pupils' feelings of competence and confidence. These aspects of the 'hidden' curriculum have direct relationships with children's learning opportunities, but they are also linked to their classroom behaviour. Children who sense that their teacher holds positive expectations about their learning potential and values them as persons are going to feel better about themselves. They will therefore feel less need to indulge in acting-out behaviour to gain status and compensate for beliefs in their inadequacy, and will feel more inclined to cooperate to demonstrate that the teacher's expectations are justified.

Teachers who are concerned about the 'management' of children's behaviour rather than just 'controlling' the class are sensitive to children's self-evaluations and will endeavour to encourage positive thinking, thus reducing the chances of children becoming alienated from schooling. These issues are taken up in Chapter 6.

Each of the approaches just described requires teachers to analyse the effects of their own behaviour on that of the children's. It is sometimes easier to stick doggedly to familiar control practices even when they are manifestly not working. For instance, some teachers continue to nag and shout at individuals or the class even though these actions are winding the pupils up and provoking more of the behaviour which teachers are trying to stamp out. By contrast, successful class managers are more prepared to engage in self-appraisal, to experiment with new approaches, and to change practices in the light of experience. They are, if you like, researchers in their own classrooms.

However, this re-appraisal is best undertaken collaboratively with colleagues rather than alone. Classroom control has traditionally been left to the intiative of individual class teachers, perhaps with the option of sending pupils to the head or other senior member of staff. The understanding has been that to seek the support of colleagues, other than by 'referring upwards' or having a moan in the staffroom, would be to signal professional incompetence. Consequently some teachers would rather be ineffective than develop skills through constructive discussion with colleagues. Teachers who are interested in improving their classroom relationships know that they have much to learn from each other and that they will receive much moral support if problems are shared. The Elton recommendation concerning peer support groups is particularly relevant here (see pp. 107–108).

Pupils' behaviour towards each other

Teachers who think in terms of 'managing behaviour' and not just 'controlling pupils' are as much concerned with the quality of relationships between their pupils as with conduct in the presence of authority figures. True, there can be management which is unfeeling and shows scant regard for individual rights and personal needs: but we tend to say that this is 'bad' management. At least at its best, the 'management' of pupil behaviour implies a concern for children's individual predicaments and welfare needs as well as the needs of the school as an institution. Control still plays an important part in regulating social behaviour because children, both as individuals and in groups, need direction: but the need to consider such issues as playground behaviour and aggression between pupils is recognised and forms part of the school's behaviour policy. In the classroom, teachers will be concerned to deepen children's understanding of their own behaviour and to facilitate opportunities in which children learn to be more cooperative. The current concern with the scale of bullying in schools (see pp. 95–103) is an example of a problem which is not adequately addressed through traditional control approaches which focus just on the institutional needs of the school. These aspects of behaviour management are discussed in Chapter 7.

Collaborative approaches

Although head teachers and governors have the overall responsibility for the school's behaviour policy, and although individual class teachers have the responsibility to keep order, the concept of managing pupil behaviour assumes that decision-making should be *shared*. The importance of teachers being willing to share perspectives and learn from each other, as mentioned earlier, is a fundamental aspect of the collaborative approach. There are three other particularly important dimensions:

(1) *The involvement of parents*

In traditional school regimes, parents are frequently involved in so far as they are told about school rules, uniform, the system of punishments and rewards. However, they have not always been *well* informed, particularly in matters affecting the behaviour of their own children. The management of pupil behaviour includes recognising parental *rights* with respect to information and opportunities for discussion, both about school policy in general and their child in particular. Parents need to have easy access to the head and to individual teachers, and they need to know that their perspective will be welcomed and treated as valid. Some schools also regard home-visiting as an integral, if time-consuming, component of effective home-school liaison.

Besides parental rights, many primary schools are trying to work with parents in a spirit of *partnership*. Parental involvement in reading and other areas of the curriculm has benefits not only in terms of children's intellectual development but also in terms of their attitude to school and motivation to learn. Parents may also be involved in behaviour matters more directly, participating with teachers in working out behaviour policy (e.g. over approaches to bullying and playground behaviour) and cooperating in the monitoring of their child's behaviour in school. These and other aspects of parental involvement will be taken up in the last chapter of this book.

not just decision making /negotiating but evaluating own behav and consequences – individual respons .

(2) *The involvement of pupils*

Although the research team appointed by the Elton Committee asked teachers to explain the behaviour problems which they faced in schools, they did not conduct any investigation to find out what the pupils thought, even at secondary level. This is surprising in view of the team's recommendation that 'headteachers and teachers should give pupils every opportunity to take responsibilities and to make a full contribution to improving behaviour in school' (p. 143). Some people argue that primary school pupils are too young to have coherent and rational views about the management of their individual and group behaviour, and that it would therefore be improper to let them have a say. This position is understandable. Even in the upper junior classes, children at this stage of schooling lack the social maturity to see problems from various points of view and to predict the consequences of their decisions.

However, there are three main reasons for believing that the gradual involvement of pupils in decisions relating to their behaviour is appropriate. The first is that it works! As we shall see at various points later in this book, provided children are given a clear framework in which to participate, they take seriously and make constructive contributions to such matters as classroom rules, playground behaviour and bullying. Some primary schools have also successfully set up School Councils to help determine general policy. Equally, those with behaviour problems are generally capable of helping to set their own behavioural targets and monitoring their own progress – provided, again, that they work within a clear structure.

The second reason is a managerial one. The Elton Report recognised that it is through eliciting their active involvement as initiators of ideas that children feel committed to policies and to the school as a community.

Thirdly, engaging children in debate about school behaviour is valuable in its own right, as part of their social and moral education. Teachers who 'manage' children's behaviour are sensitive to the children's perception of rules and their justification because they want to develop pupils' *understanding* of rules and the part they play in regulating individual freedom, in protecting minority interests, and in promoting the common good. These notions do not just come naturally to children, but arise through their interactions with peers and adults and through experiencing the consequences of decision-making. Involving pupils also contributes to children's emotional development, helping them to refine their feelings about their own and others' behaviour problems.

The role of adults in eliciting the involvement of children in behavioural matters, far from being peripheral, is central. Young children need help in identifying issues, in formulating and explaining their ideas, in listening to each other, in discussing the usefulness of their suggestions and in thinking of ways in which they can be put into practice. When ideas do not work out as expected, they also need constructive support about 'what to do now'.

(3) *Whole-school policies*

We saw earlier that the systems model of pupil behaviour involves the notion of numerous *interacting* elements. This being so, it follows that changing any one element in the school system could have implications for other elements. For example, a change to staggered playtimes to alleviate playground problems has implications for the lengths of lessons, which in turn has implications for curriculum opportunities, which in turn could have implications for pupil behaviour. Hence it is essential that there are whole-school policies which take account of the uniqueness of the school's situation and the inter-relatedness of the elements which make up that situation.

The author recently asked a primary head if she had a whole-school policy for behaviour. 'Oh yes, indeed,' came the reply, 'I wrote it during the summer holidays'. The policy document was certainly comprehensive and positive, and it had been submitted to the staff for their consideration. Nonetheless, for all the amendments and fine tuning, it was regarded essentially as the head's instructions. A genuine whole-school policy is not only *about* the whole school but is *drawn up by* the whole school. This involves the active participation of all the pupils and all the staff, while other members of the school community – non-teaching staff, parents, governors – should also be invited to make a contribution. Management in this context certainly includes leadership from the head, but it is the kind of leadership which arrests apathy, sets up the mechanisms for discussion, delegates coordinating responsibilities, facilitates the communication and exchange of ideas between different parts of the school community, and engenders an attitude of mind which encourages everyone to consider ideas no matter how much they challenge the school's time-honoured approaches (or lack of approaches!).

The process by which a whole-school policy emerges should be such that each contributor learns something from the experience, gaining a deeper understanding of the issues and developing a sense of ownership about the emerging policies. These issues will be explored in Chapter 8.

Chapter 3

Forestalling Behaviour Problems

> We conclude that the central problem of disruption could be
> significantly reduced by helping teachers to become more effective
> classroom managers.
>
> *Elton Report, p. 12*

From the evidence cited in the previous chapter, it seems that teachers
who are successful in manging children's behaviour are those who,
among other things, adopt two mutually supporting approaches. One
involves anticipating the kind of circumstances when problem behaviour could arise and taking preventive measures. Trying to cope by
using strategies which come into play only when incidents occur does
not constitute sound management practice. The other approach
involves taking measures to reinforce the behaviour wanted. This is
more effective than concentrating most of the time on trying to
eliminate the behaviour that is not wanted. In this chapter and the next
we examine some practical strategies associated with each of these
approaches, starting in the present chapter with those concerned with
pre-empting misbehaviour.

Classroom rules

Rules are integral to the well-being of any institution. In his study of
pupils' perceptions of rules, Cullingford (1988) shows clearly that by
the time children reach the end of their primary education they take the
need for rules for granted. Whilst some children may feel that teachers
sometimes unfairly *apply* rules of behaviour, they do not question the
principle that schools must have rules. As one top junior boy put it, 'If
we didn't have school rules, this place would be upside down'.

Apart from those which govern general behaviour in the school,
rules for the classroom constitute one way of pre-empting misbehav-

iour. They help to establish a framework in which children are helped to understand what counts as acceptable and unacceptable conduct. Classroom rules also give a set of criteria for acceptable behaviour to which teachers can easily and regularly refer.

In developing rules for the classroom, the teacher needs to address a number of issues. What should the rules be about? How many rules should there be? How should they be formulated? Should they be imposed, or should the children have a say? How should they be communicated and enforced?

As regards the first of these questions, classroom rules need to serve three overlapping needs:

- to ensure safety and personal welfare;
- to provide effective conditions for teaching and learning;
- to help children develop considerate behaviour and respect for property.

Hence rules often cover the following Issues:

- entering, leaving and moving around the room;
- handling materials and equipment;
- talking and listening;
- treating others as you would like them to treat you;
- making the room a pleasant place to be in.

It helps if formal classroom rules are few in number, say, four or five. This not only makes it easier for children to remember them but also minimises the risk of endless reprimand. The more rules you have, the more possible their infringment!

Some teachers believe that it is better to have just one or two rules which lay down general principles rather than specify precise behaviour. A rule such as 'We will try to treat others as we want to be treated ourselves' would come into this category. These kinds of rules have the advantage of providing a framework for all eventualities, encouraging children to empathise with their peers and prompting them to think about the consequences of their behaviour.

However, there are limits to how far children will achieve orderly classroom conduct without also the help of precise rules for everyday matters such as movement and talking. Primary school children, especially the younger ones, need specific guidance to encourage the development of good habits. A suitable compromise, especially for juniors, is to have one rule which provides general criteria and additionally a small number of specific rules which, in effect, give

28

practical application to the general guidelines and draw attention to matters of particular importance.

positive realistic

Pupils like to know where they are, and it is therefore important, on first meeting a class, for the teacher to make explicit the kind of behaviour that will be expected. Taking care over the way in which rules are worded will help pupils to observe them more regularly. A lengthy list of 'must nots' encourages defiance. Constructive relationships with the children are more likely to be promoted if the rules are generally phrased in terms of the behaviour wanted rather than the behaviour not wanted. It also helps if rules are phrased as communal commitments rather than imposed imperatives. For example, 'We will listen carefully when the teacher is speaking' would be preferable to 'No talking when the teacher is speaking'. For some matters, particularly those affecting safety, an assertive wording is needed, but for others such as silence during individual tasks, when total compliance on the part of young children might be an unreasonable expectation, wording to represent the importance of effort sets more realistic objectives and appears more manageable. For example: 'We will try hard to be quiet when working on our own'.

The nature of classroom rules and the procedure for establishing them will vary from one age group to another. Here, a teacher in an inner-city school, explains what she does with her reception class:

> Most children at this age won't have experienced a large group, so we need rules to help them work happily without squabbling. For example, in my class we have a rule to regulate the number of children who can engage in any one activity. We say, 'Only two should be in the home corner, only two with the sand or water, only three with the lego or train, and so on'. This is important because it pre-empts hassle. Then we have a rule about being tidy: 'We will put things away where we found them'. A third rule concerns noise levels: 'We will try to be very quiet in the book corner'. We don't have a general 'no talking' rule because for some things, like the home corner, talk is needed. Making silence specific to the book corner helps children to learn when talking would hinder them and when it is appropriate. I also make it clear that there is one occasion when I must not be interrupted, and that is when I am sharing reading with a child. When I introduce rules and issue reminders, I'm always careful to discuss the rationale so that children understand why the rule is needed.

As children move through the junior years, teachers can increasingly engage them in discussion about the kinds of rules which are needed to meet the needs of the class. Practise in rule-making contributes to pupils' social education. The process of discussion, explaining, justifying and revising suggestions, helps to generate understanding and a positive attitude towards rules. Left to their own devices, younger juniors especially will tend to suggest negative and imperative statements, with plenty of 'must nots' and 'don'ts'. The teacher therefore needs to provide a clear framework which helps the class identify key issues, prioritise them, and formulate them in terms of the behaviour wanted rather than not wanted.

With her class of 7- to 8-year-olds, one teacher was observed proceeding on the following lines. She began by writing on the board 'What would make our class a happy and nice place to be in?', and asking for suggestions. After a free exchange of ideas, the teacher focussed on certain issues which had emerged in the discussion, and wrote these on the board using the children's formulations: 'not talking when working', 'not running', 'listening carefully', 'keeping the room tidy'. She then asked the class to suggest how the first two could be worded 'so that we all know what to do'. Following the children's suggestions, these were changed to 'working quietly' and 'moving quietly'. The teacher then set the class some writing centred on the stimulus question on the board, and some children read out what they had written. She later used the children's ideas to make a poster, which read:

> Keeping our class a happy place
> a. We will try to work quietly so as not to disturb others.
> b. We will listen carefully when the teacher is talking to us.
> c. We will move quietly round the room, and walk.
> d. We will put litter in the bin.

By the time children are in the upper junior classes, they are able to take more initiative themselves. This is how one teacher explains how she organised rule-making with her 10- to 11-year-olds in a series of stages:

1. The children were put in groups of four and given ten minutes to devise a set of rules which we all had to follow.
2. We then collated the ideas, which I listed on the board. At this stage, no one was allowed to comment.
3. Then, back in their groups, the children were asked to prioritise the rules. We found ten that were common to most groups.
4. The whole class then voted for the five rules they thought were the most important. In the event, these centred round the concept of 'respect', so we decided on one general rule – 'We will show respect for each other' – to introduce the specific rules.
5. With a group of five children during an activity period, we talked about the way the rules could be worded, and two of the children

then made a poster which we put up on the wall. This was headed by the general rule and then the specific ones, which were:

We will show respect for each other by

a. Speaking one at a time
b. Listening carefully to each other and the teacher
c. Respecting each other's possessions (This included me respecting their possessions, for instance not taking something from someone's tray without first asking.)
d. Each being responsible for keeping the room tidy.
e. Voting on ways of working in groups when we can't agree.

Opportunities should also be taken to revise rules as needs and circumstances change. This helps children to learn to regard a set of rules as a flexible instrument which can be altered by agreement to meet personal and institutional needs more effectively. The children's involvement in rule-making should not therefore amount to a one-off activity, but one which is constantly maintained as the utility of the rules is monitored.

Children need regular reminders about classroom rules. The skill involved here is reminding without reprimanding. Of course there is a place for reprimanding (see Chapter 5), but constant bickering will almost certainly be resented and lead to a deterioration in classroom relationships. The Junior School Project (Mortimore *et al.* 1988) found behaviour to be better in classes where teachers managed to be firm without continual intervention and nagging. For not only does perpetual telling-off create general frustration and an unpleasant atmosphere, it reinforces young children's natural tendency to think of rules as adult impositions, the purpose of obeying them being to avoid the adult's displeasure. Successful management of pupil behaviour depends on creating a positive climate in which children do not just try to keep on good terms with the teacher but understand that observing rules helps to provide a better atmosphere for learning and make the classroom a happier place.

How, then, can children be reminded about rules of behaviour without resorting to regular reprimanding? One way is to display the rules and discuss them periodically, particularly just before the start of activities to which they especially apply. The author observed a junior school teacher reminding the class about a rule concerning retrieval of resources before they embarked on group projects, and noted how careful she was to draw attention to the fact that the rule had been drawn up collaboratively: 'You remember that we agreed that . . .'. In another room, the reception class teacher was carefully rehearsing the rule pertaining to using paints and brushes as she started an art activity. Here it was interesting to see how the reminding ended on a positive note: 'Now go and enjoy yourselves'.

A second 'reminding' strategy is to include rules and their justification as part of normal teaching. For instance, the teacher could remind children of a listening rule as she starts to explain or instruct. She might say: 'Now, listen carefully everyone so that you all know what to do', or 'When everyone is ready we can all enjoy the story', or 'Attend carefully now because I want to explain this'.

Thirdly, it is important to praise children who are observing the rules, being careful to specify the conduct to which you are drawing attention (see p. 49). The effect is to send round the room a 'ripple effect', other children too getting the message.

Kounin 1970

see Saunders

Lesson planning

Effective lesson planning includes pre-empting behaviour problems which could occur through the children being bored, confused or frustrated. Boredom can arise when children are insufficiently stimulated or challenged, or are left too long on a particular task, or are given insufficient feedback about their progress. Confusion can occur if children are not clear what is expected of them or how to proceed or what to do next. Frustration can ensue if the task is too difficult or insufficient, or if the materials and books are not easily accessible.

A characteristic of good classroom managers is that they engender an atmosphere of *purposefulness*. The children feel challenged and know what is expected of them and are given the means to achieve these expectations. The following checklist and comments indicate some of the ways in which effective lesson preparation can maximise feelings of purposefulness and so reduce the occasion for misbehaviour.

(1) *Are the pupils being given plenty to do and a variety of activities?*

An important finding in the Junior School Project was that the better-behaved classes tended to be those in which there was an unmistakable atmosphere of work. By this was not meant busyness for its own sake ('keeping them occupied'), but purposeful busyness which arose from feeling actively involved in realistically demanding tasks. In these circumstances pupils enjoyed their work more, were more eager to start new activities, made less noise, and moved around the room less often and more sensibly.

One way of achieving variety is to ensure that, over the course of a week, and to some extent the day and each session, the children are engaged in tasks which vary in respects such as the following:

– Different *task demands* (e.g. practice items; problem-solving; making and testing suggestions; tasks requiring imagination)
– Different *modes of working* (e.g. reading; writing; practical work; physical activity; discussion)
– Different *sources of stimulus* (e.g. questions posed by the teacher – closed and open; explanations by the teacher; books; worksheets; stories; pictures; objects; living things; audio tapes; video; overhead projector; visiting speakers)
– Different *opportunities for pupil interaction* (e.g. working individually; in pairs; small groups)
– Different *demands on pupils' initiative* (e.g. tasks which are highly structured by the teacher, somewhat structured, or leave much room for choice)
– Different *audiences for whom work is produced* (e.g. the teacher, the class, the school, parents).

Variety can be achieved both within and between these groupings.

In some classrooms, variety is provided through the provision of diverse activities all going on at once. However, another finding in the Junior School Project was that behaviour was better in classes which were engaged in not more than two or three different curriculum areas at any one time. This enabled the teacher to focus more easily on topic rather than organisational matters; it also facilitated class discussion, listening skills, and the sharing of ideas. This does not mean that teachers should assiduously avoid multi-task sessions, which they may regard as important in facilitating choice and flexibility; but it does suggest that special skills in organisation are needed. In particular, care needs to be taken so that the various groups do not all need the teacher's help at once.

(2) *Have the necessary materials been identified and easy access to them arranged?*

Purposefulness in the classroom presupposes that children have ready access to the materials they need. Some classrooms are divided into resource and activity areas which reduces dependence on the teacher. There might be a writing area, a book corner, an art and craft section, a maths section, and so on. But for lessons when the whole class is engaged in the same sort of activity, the key materials are best set out on the children's tables before the class arrives. Alternatively, a resource table can be placed in the centre of the room.

If the teacher has to spend time giving out materials, or if children are needing to cross the room to get what they want, opportunity for misbehaviour is created. Having everything ready and easily accessible helps to generate the right mood by providing a work-centred environment from the start and focussing children's attention on the activity as soon as they enter the room.

(3) *Has special care been taken in planning the first ten minutes of the lesson?*

The beginning of the morning and afternoon has sometimes to be taken up with administrative tasks. For instance, the teacher may be calling the register, accounting for absentees, asking about missing homework, dealing with individual problems, or collecting money. There needs to be a well-understood procedure which allows the children to be constructively occupied while they are waiting. Some administrative matters can perhaps be dealt with later in the lesson when the class is working. The beginning of the lesson can then be more work-focussed and get off to a quick start.

It helps to establish a routine procedure for the start of sessions. Here is what one infant teacher does for the period following breaktime:

> They come back chatting and excited with perhaps one or two tearful because something unpleasant has occurred in the playground. So we decided that after play they should come in and sit quietly on the carpet. We're together then as a group. I chat about personal matters, perhaps asking if they've had a nice play, and trying to calm anyone who has been upset by what another child has said or done. Then I remind them what we were doing before play and we discuss the activities we are going to do now. This gives everyone a chance to breath, and we all know where we are.

(4) *Has thought been given to the supervision of group work and children's different curriculum needs?*

The organisation of group work needs especially careful planning. A guide issues by the School Examinations and Assessment Council (1990) identifies three basic modes of working:

A. The class is engaged within one area, say Mathematics, but the children are working in three or four groups. Each group has a task which has been chosen to match the level of achievement of the group members. In this way the curriculum is differentiated. The teacher may begin by briefing the whole class. She then intends to spread her attention among the groups, as well as being available to individual children.

B. Here a class is divided into groups engaged on three or four quite different activities as a contribution to a balanced curriculum. The teacher plans to make a major commitment to one particular group, while maintaining light supervision over the others.

C. In this class many of the children are working at activities they have chosen themselves. The teacher might well support children in an individual way.

An important part of lesson planning is therefore deciding which method of working would be the most appropriate to use, and planning accordingly. The golden rule should be never to organise a lesson so that each group needs the teacher all the time. Only the second mode of working listed above specifically caters for this. The assumption in the other modes is that supervision demands will not be too demanding: don't ask what they can't deliver! Special provision needs to be made for pupils who have been absent, particularly when this means that they have missed the introduction to a new learning activity.

(5) *Has thought been given to the most appropriate way of helping children who are working individually?*

In some classrooms, the teacher visits children at their tables, supervising, marking and responding to those who have their hands up. In other classrooms, the teacher deals with individuals who queue at her desk. A dual-queuing system is sometimes found, the teacher hearing children read on one side of the desk whilst helping and marking on the other. A compromise arrangement between the 'I come to you' and 'You come to me' pattern of working involves the teacher attending to individuals in a mobile queue as she circulates to supervise the rest of the class.

The evidence about the relative efficiency of these different management strategies is equivocal, and all seem to have problems. In one study of infant classrooms, West and Wheldall (1989) found that children had to wait less time when the teacher operated a queue system. Another finding was that in 'hands up' classrooms requests could be missed when the teacher scanned the room because some children found it difficult to keep their arm raised. However, queues create conditions for misbehaviour by requiring children to move out of their seat and wait with nothing to do. Sitting behind a desk may also make the teacher seem physically remote to small children, whereas moving round the room helps to establish physical closeness. Bennett *et al.* (1984) also argue that queues make it difficult for the teacher to spot general difficulties. They found that teachers attending to queues building up at their desk failed to appreciate the scale of misunderstanding in the class or adequately diagnose learning problems. This seems a crucial point. On the other hand, as West and Wheldall (1989) point out, teachers who circulate are not necessarily any better at checking for general problems if they are preoccupied with responding to 'hands up' enquiries.

The presence of parent helpers and support staff contribute to resolving these problems, but even so four matters remain clearly important. One is to ensure that previous instruction, the nature of the task and the resources available are such that there should be no need for lots of children to require help at once. This frees the teacher to supervise, encourage, detect difficulties and diagnose problems. Secondly, for low-level requests such as spellings there must be well-understood self-help procedures which allow the teacher to use her time more effectively. Thirdly, teachers should suspend helping individuals periodically and circulate to ensure that general misunderstandings or learning problems are not going undetected. Lastly, teachers should consider reducing the amount of time in which the whole class engages in individual tasks and make greater use of the 'B' group system in item 5 above, whereby one group is taught and the others need minimal intervention. Bennett *et al.* (1984) argue that this style of classroom organisation represents the most efficient use of the teacher's time, allowing more opportunity than other modes of working for teacher-pupil and pupil-pupil interaction.

(6) *Has thought been given to ways of managing critical points in the lesson*?

Critical points in lessons are those where the nature of the event makes the risk of misbehaviour high. Examples are:

- explaining what the children are going to do
- getting an activity started
- putting children into groups

- dealing with children finishing at different times
- ending one kind of activity and beginning another
- preparing the class to move to a different room
- re-arranging furniture
- putting away materials and equipment
- ending the lesson.

In a study of teachers of 11-year-olds, Doyle and Carter (1987) found that misbehaviour occurs most readily during the time when the activities are beginning. The mistake is to start to help individual pupils before ensuring that the class in general has understood what needs to be done and is able to get started. Not only is it very important to take great care over the initial instructions, but also – especially when getting to know a class – to move round the room quickly to check for general problems *before* spending time with those individuals who need sustained help.

It is not surprising if restlessness and frustration develop when children are not clear about what is expected of them. Teachers at the start of their career would find it helpful to *rehearse* carefully what they want to say when introducing an activity, forestalling possible teaching difficulties such as asking the right sort of introductory questions or getting over a complicated point. It is a safe bet that pupils will finish (or maintain they have!) at different times. The programme of work needs to cater for this inevitable eventuality so that everyone is clear what to do when they have completed a task.

Noise levels and behaviour problems can easily build up at the ends of lessons and at points of transition from one activity to the next. It is particularly critical when pupils have to move to another part of the school, if furniture has to be put back, if paints and messy materials have to be put away, or if equipment has to be returned to a store or another classroom. If, in the event, too much time is left, that is all to the good since the opportunity can be used for drawing the class together for general feedback, or a story or some other activity that helps the children to feel members of the group.

(7) *Has sufficient opportunity been provided for feedback and discussion about the pupils' work?*

It is a common fault with beginning teachers to allow children to work for so long on their own that they become restless. A class needs to be pulled together at intervals to provide feedback, to reinforce what has been learned and provide further stimulus. One reception class teacher told the author: 'When things look as if they are going to get bubbly, we sit down on the carpet together and discuss what everybody has being doing and what we should do next'. A junior class teacher in the same school said: 'When the first signs of restlessness appear, I call the class together. We *share* what we've achieved and the problems we've come up against, and so become one family again'.

The Junior School Project found that behaviour is better in classes where the teacher sets aside time to talk about what pupils have been doing. Children need to feel that what they have accomplished is appropriate and that any difficulties they have experienced are being addressed. General class feedback also gives opportunity to share work and ideas and discuss follow-up tasks and homework.

(8) *Have discussion sessions been prepared so that as many pupils as possible can be actively involved?*

Good behaviour and effective learning are promoted when each individual feels a significant member of the group. One aspect of helping children to feel that they 'belong' is to ensure that as many as possible make a contribution to class discussion. It is important to prepare questions very carefully, paying attention to their sequencing, the precise way each is phrased, and ensuring that children are not only asked to recall facts but also invited to suggest ideas and give their opinions. This is not only educationally important but gives the less well-informed children more opportunity to respond and receive positive recognition. It is also good for the children's self-esteem to know that their views are being sought.

The manner of inviting responses is also important. It helps to: pause and look round before calling on a child; name children from different parts of the room; ensure that the same group do not monopolise the discussion while the rest of the class feel left out or choose to opt out; allow children time to make a response; and give cues and rephrase questions to help children along.

Body language and use of voice

Studies of young children's perceptions of classroom management strategies indicate that, in the eyes of the pupils, 'good' teachers are those who are at once firm, friendly and fair, who take an interest in individuals but also 'help you to learn' (Davies, 1979). Children feel more secure with teachers who manage to be assertive without being domineering, and who are prepared to be flexible without being indecisive in their actions. In these respects the use of both verbal and non-verbal language is all-important.

To achieve the status of authority with a class, it is necessary for the teacher to *communicate confidence*. With some teachers, classroom management suffers from conflicting, paradoxical communication. One message is carried by the words and another by the tone of voice, facial expression and posture. To give the impression of assurance, it is important that uncertainty is not betrayed in one's non-verbal language.

Use of voice

Hesitant speech conveys uncertainty and may leave the children confused about what they should do. Beginning teachers can help themselves by preparing essential instructions carefully so that they know just what they want to say and how to put it across. When addressing the class the voice needs to be projected, but without shouting. Maintaining a loud voice signals the message 'I'm not really in control of the situation'. At the same time, modulating the voice helps to convey the point and maintain interest. It pays off to use a tape-recorder to listen to oneself addressing the class: does the voice sound apologetic, or whiny, or timid, or sarcastic, or aggressive? Has the voice a little bit of fun in it, or is it deadpan and humourless? The recorder can then be used to practise modulating the voice so that it conveys interest, warmth and confidence.

An important aspect of voice control relates to times when it is necessary to gain everybody's attention. A common experience for beginning teachers is to find themselves shouting 'Be quiet!' and, on gaining little response, continuing to raise their voice whilst becoming increasingly agitated. Unfortunately children find this great entertainment! How can this predicament be avoided?

One strategy is to pre-empt the problem by agreeing a standard phrase or signal which the class understands to mean that everyone must stop and look towards the teacher, turning their chairs if necessary. Children sometimes show remarkable ingenuity in suggesting appropriate signals for the teacher to use when calling the class to attention, but a simple announcement such as 'Will everybody listen' or 'Stop and look this way' would do.

If the class does not respond to a request to listen, it is often effective to direct the remark to one or two named individuals: 'Peter, I would like you to look this way, please. [Pause and look to another individual.] And you, Sharon – put that away so that we can begin'. [Pause and scan the room] Right, now, everybody listen carefully so you know what to do.'

A similar strategy which can often be even more effective is to make a *positive* statement about a particular individual or group. A second year junior teacher was recently observed gaining total silence in a rather rowdy classroom by fixing her gaze on a group of the better-behaved children and saying, 'My goodness! *That* table is sitting up really nicely!'.

Posture

The way teachers hold themselves says a lot about their confidence and how they feel about their authority. Indeed, as we know from every-day experience, we can make ourselves feel more confident by taking a deep breath and standing up straight. When addressing the whole class, anxiety, tension, and submissiveness is conveyed by standing with hunched shoulders, clasping arms in front of the body or having them folded, leaning on a table supported by outstretched fingers, and standing against the wall away from the children. It is usually best to stand relaxed but erect with limbs placed evenly, and hands loosely by the side or gesturing a little to reinforce the meaning of what is being said. It helps also to move into the group sometimes to reduce social distance. When helping individuals, it appears less threatening if the teacher squats or draws up a chair and sits by the child, since eye contact is then on the same level.

Facial expression and eye contact

Of all aspects of body language, smiling and maintaining eye contact are perhaps the most important. Neill (1989) found that while children of all ages regard teachers who smile as friendly, cheerful and inter-esting, and those who frown as unfriendly, bad-tempered and boring, younger children are particularly influenced by these facial expressions.

Successful relationships depend upon knowing how the other person is reacting, and for this we depend upon 'semantic signals' given by the eyes, facial expression and head movements. By nodding, smiling and maintaining eye contact while a child is speaking, a teacher helps to reassure and convey the message that she is following what is being said. When addressing the whole class or talking to a group, it is obviously impossible to sustain eye contact with everyone at the same time! However it is important to look directly at the children, focussing on different parts of the room and different individuals in turn. When pupils are responding, the teacher should avoid averting her gaze by glancing downwards or away since this gives the appearance of disinterestedness.

Engendering work involvement

As we saw earlier, an important conclusion in the Junior School Project was that better-behaved classes are those in which the teacher generates a work-centred atmosphere. This relates well to Jacob Kounin's studies of teachers' classroom management skills, which concern ways in which teachers can engender a high level of work involvement and thereby create conditions in which misbehaviour is less likely to occur.

In his observations of classes of 5- to 11-year-olds, Kounin identified a number of strategies which help to keep children 'on task'. These he called 'withitness', 'overlapping', 'alerting and accountability cues', 'smoothness' and 'momentum'.

A teacher displays *withitness*, or vigilance, by giving the impression that she has eyes at the back of her head. Beginning teachers especially sometimes become so engrossed in helping a group or individual that they fail to notice what is going on somewhere else in the room. Noise levels and misbehaviour are then allowed to develop, and the teacher finds herself scolding and shouting, yet unsure on whom to pin the blame.

When talking to an individual or group, it is therefore essential to take up a position so that as much of the room as possible comes within one's field of vision, and then to glance up to scan the class quickly at regular intervals. If it is known that the teacher does this, the children will be less likely to misbehave since the chances of detection are high. The teacher is not only well-placed to identify the culprit correctly but to intervene before the situation escalates, preferably positively (see p. 63).

A teacher who has developed the skill of *overlapping* is able to deal with two matters at the same time. For instance, whilst hearing a child read she might look up to deal with a query briefly or unfussily coax another pupil back to work.

Alerting cues are signals to keep everyone involved. For instance, the teacher might ask a question and then pause to look round before asking someone to respond. *Accountability cues* entail periodic checks on individual progress by making public requests to individuals without being bossy. Thus a teacher might say, 'Now Darren, could you just hold your work up so I can see how much you've done...good', or 'We're going to stop in ten minutes so that we can hear what different groups have found out', or 'Tracey, I think you should now be helping Karen with the class newspaper'. Keeping children accountable for their performance is an integral part of effective teaching. If overdone, children feel rushed and coerced; but if carried out gently and in good humour, the children benefit by being given regular reminders about what is expected of them.

Smoothness and momentum are about keeping up the flow of work. Certain sorts of teacher actions interrupt the pace of the lesson and leave children confused or frustrated. The main ones, each of which Kounin supplied with a picturesque label, are as follows:

> *Thrusts*: An insensitive 'bursting in' on an activity with a peremptory order or question without any regard for what the individual or group is doing.
>
> *Dangles*: Starting one activity and leaving it 'dangling' in mid-air by an intrusive question about another matter: e.g. beginning to read a story and then stopping to ask why a child is absent, or telling off a child about a minor matter whilst trying to explain a tricky point.
>
> *Flip-flops*: Going back to an activity which has only just been stopped: e.g. 'Right , put away your maths books now. We're going to have a story. Oh, I forgot to set you some homework – can you get your books out again?'
>
> *Overdwelling*: Unnecessarily going on and on about something: e.g. nagging about not having a sharp pencil when a child is trying to concentrate on how to borrow in subtraction, or spending a long time reprimanding children for not wearing the correct PE kit when the class is waiting to start an activity.

Classroom layout and pupil grouping

It used to be common for pupils to sit in rows, but this practice is now fairly rare at primary level, though it persists in many secondary schools. The Junior School Project found row arrangements in only 10 per cent of classrooms. The Plowden Report in 1967 advised primary school teachers to place children in small groups round tables on the grounds that this would facilitate constructive interaction. Problem-solving discussion would be promoted, and, in the case of mixed-ability tables, low-achieving children would benefit by being seated with the more able. However, whether these work benefits are realised has been called into question by recent observation studies in classroom management. The work of Bennett *et al*. (1984) in infant classrooms and the ORACLE Study (Galton *et al*. 1980) with juniors showed that, typically, children sit in groups but work individually. In the latter study, as many as nine out of ten teachers at no time involved children in genuine collaborative work.

Granted that children spend much time working on individual tasks, what seating arrangements are best for promoting high work involvement and good behaviour? In a recent review of several experimental studies which addressed this question, Wheldall and Glynn (1989) reached the following conclusions:

1. Children who are accustomed to sitting round tables keep 'on task' for significantly longer periods and behave better when they are seated in rows.
2. When children who are sitting in rows return to sitting round tables their work-involvement is significantly less.
3. Children in rows produce more work and of better quality.
4. The better results in rows persists over many weeks, suggesting that the explanation is not due to the novelty of a new classroom arrangement.
5. Teachers give more praise and reprimand less in row settings.
6. For carrying out individual tasks, children express a preference for rows.

The authors explain these results by pointing to the fact that tables give children the opportunity to tease, punch each other, and kick neighbours under the table. By contrast, row formations promote better behaviour for individual tasks because there is less eye contact between pupils; and since behaviour is better, the teacher finds it easier to make favourable comments.

What practical conclusions should be drawn from these studies? Some teachers would argue that, in spite of the findings, they would prefer to stick with tables because the feeling of 'belonging' that they encourage is important for primary-aged children. However, Wheldall and Glynn are not advocating permanent row arrangements, but flexibility in furniture layout to encourage the kind of behaviour appropriate to the task. In fact, Rosenfield *et al*. (1985) demosntrated that for class discussion it is more productive to have the children seated in a circle rather than round tables, and *least* satisfactory to have the children sitting in rows. Indeed, for trust-building activities, teachers are usually advised to sit the children in a circle since this encourages an atmosphere of openness.

Shifting furniture about to suit different kinds of activities could in itself create behaviour problems, of course, but some teachers manage to arrange different parts of the classroom to suit a specific learning style. One area might consist of tables for group work, another separate study places for individual work, a third a free space for drama or sitting informally for a story or in a circle for discussion. In classrooms for infants and young juniors, the opportunity to create a family atmosphere for part of the day is facilitated by a carpeted area where children can be physically close and the teacher adopt a quieter and more friendly voice.

If classroom layout needs to take account of the nature of different activities and learning styles, so does the composition of groups. Many teachers find it best to have base groups in which the children are seated according to friendships, and to vary the composition of 'task groups' to suit the purpose of the activity. Pollard and Tann (1988) suggest that grouping children according to ability is divisive if permanent, but could be appropriate for some sorts of activity, as could grouping based on interests or friendships. There is also evidence that having permanent ability groups depresses low-attainers' perceptions of their competencies (see p. 76), and that with older primary children groups of three consisting of one high-attainer and two low-attainers helps to promote cooperative learning (see p.104–105). The Wheldall and Glynn review indicated that mixed-sex seating produced greater work involvement and lower rates of disruption. This tends to support the practice of some teachers who place boys and girls together to discourage misbehaviour. However, most teachers would not want to force this 'unnatural' arrangement on the whole class all the time.

Lastly, children like to be consulted about their room and to discuss what arrangements are the most helpful to them. As Coulby and Coulby (1990) point out, children are more likely to respect their classroom if they are involved in decisions about its layout, maintenance and the display areas since this encourages the class to accept communal ownership.

Chapter 4

Promoting Good Behaviour

> While some schools seem preoccupied with bad behaviour, others have
> concerted policies for raising expectations and improving standards.
> The schools we saw which had such positive policies ... had
> marginalised bad behaviour by promoting good behaviour.
>
> *Elton Report, p. 66.*

Research in British classrooms reveals that, above the infant stage,
teachers are sparing in their use of praise and approval. In the Junior
School Project, (Mortimore *et al.*, 1988) for instance, it was found that
teachers on average spent less than 1 per cent of their time commenting
favourably on children's work or behaviour. They were also found to
criticise unwanted behaviour far more frequently than they praised
good behaviour, a finding which also emerged in the ORACLE study
of 58 top junior classrooms in three local authorities (Galton *et al.*
1980).

It seems that teachers assume children 'ought' to behave well, and
that good behaviour does not therefore 'deserve' to be praised. In the
Junior School Project, a few teachers of older juniors expressed the
view that giving praise generously could lead to 'inflation' and be
devalued by the pupils. Whilst recognising an element of truth in this,
the researchers considered, after many hours of classroom observation, that most teachers could afford to praise much more and to
criticise much less.

In one of the few British studies which has focussed specially on this
topic, Merrett and Wheldall (1986) made separate recordings of rates
of approval for work and social behaviour in the classrooms of 128
teachers in primary and middle schools. Taking account of teachers'
facial expressions and gestures as well as what they said to pupils, it
was found that approval was communicated three times more often
than disapproval when the focus was on pupils' academic endeavours.
However, when the subject for comment was the children's social
behaviour, disapproval was expressed five times more often than

approval. In fact almost three out of ten teachers never praised for good behaviour at any time they were observed! Evidence of this kind led the Elton Committee to comment:

> We are left with the disturbing impression that in some schools a pupil can only get attention in one or other of two ways - by working well or by behaving badly. (p.99)

As Merrett and Wheldall (1986) suggest, teachers probably find it reinforcing to correct unacceptable behaviour, partly because they like to think that they are successful in detecting it and partly because their reprimands may have a favourable short-term impact. However, unlike praise, reprimanding does nothing directly to promote good behaviour, though it may be combined with statements which specify what is expected.

Using praise effectively

According to Brophy (1981), who conducted a definitive review of American research, it is just as well that many teachers refrain from praising since praise is frequently ineffective and even counter-productive! The dangers are most likely when teachers praise just for encouragement, or praise in too general a way without specifying what the praise is for. There is no doubt, however, as Brophy himself shows, that a *discriminating* use of praise can have a potent effect on children's motivation to work better and behave well. It is therefore important for teachers to be sensitive to the *conditions* in which praise is most likely to be effective.

So what is it that teachers need to do in order to make optimal use of praise? This is not an easy question to answer because the evidence from research is often equivocal. The age of the child, whether the recipient is a boy or a girl, and whether the praise is for work or conduct, are among the variables which make generalisations difficult. Also, much of the evidence comes from carefully controlled experiments, and these have sometimes yielded different findings from observation studies in regular classrooms where praise is less systematic. The following suggestions should therefore be regarded as general guiding principles rather than tips to follow in all eventualities.

(1) *Use praise generously with infants and young juniors, but be more discriminating with older primary children.*

Developmental studies have shown that up to the age of seven or eight, the desire to please adults is a powerful influence on children's behaviour. Infants seem to have an insatiable appetite for praise, which provides them with authoritative guidance and feedback as well as encouragement. Older juniors, however, are often more concerned about receiving approval from their peers than their teachers. For them, praise therefore needs to be used in a more discriminating way.

Young children also seem to respond to praise particularly well when the teacher's non-verbal behaviour reinforces her verbal remarks. Wheldall *et al.* (1986) report evidence which shows that praise accompanied by touch helps to reinforce appropriate behaviour in infant classrooms. In two experiments, they found that touch used in conjunction with statements of approval led to significantly greater levels of concentration and a reduction in disruptive behaviour. The authors argue that non-verbal factors, of which touch is one, help to convey the teacher's commendation by heightening the emotional climate.

This may present a dilemma for some school staff, who feel that the risk of accusations of child abuse demand a 'no touching' policy. However, whilst acknowledging the need to be aware of the danger of false allegations, Michele Elliott, Director of Kidscape (an organisation set up to prevent child abuse), believes it is professionally important for teachers to respond to young children's need for physical contact. This view is also taken by Professor Richard Whitfield of the National Family Trust (Purcheon, 1990).

(2) *Catch the child being good*

Praise is an invaluable means of emphasising the importance of behaving well as opposed to not behaving badly. Yet with some children the frequency of problem behaviour may make it difficult to praise legitimately. One has therefore to *look out* for good behaviour, or, as is sometimes said, to 'catch the child being good'. This requires vigilance to avoid missing opportunities for showing approval. This is all the more effective when the classroom rules have been negotiated with the children and regularly discussed, since the class is then particularly sensitive to the kinds of behaviour which will earn praise.

(3) *Give praise early*

One of the reasons why many children benefit from computer programmes is that they obtain reinforcement as soon as they make a correct response. In a classroom, however, children often have to wait a long time before the teacher attends to them and is in a position to express approval for their work. In the ORACLE project referred to earlier, the average amount of individual attention which a child received during the course of a week was only 35 minutes.

In laboratory conditions, it has been shown that the teachers' effective use of praise is dependent on praising contingently and immediately, that is, reinforcing specific target behaviours, and only those behaviours, as soon as these are demonstrated. However, this is not easy for teachers who have not received training in behavioural methods. As Brophy (1981) explains, 'Teachers dealing with classes of 25 or 30 students are not even going to notice all of the relevant specific behaviours that students perform, let alone to reinforce them effectively' (p. 20).

It is important, therefore, to devise a strategy which takes account of classroom constraints. The aim should be to 'catch children being good', both as regards work and behaviour, as *early* as possible in a lesson. It is sometimes tempting to begin a session in a negative manner by delivering public criticisms about behaviour or work. Children will often protest against such scolding, particularly if they think the criticism is unjustified or if it is typical of the teacher's management style. The class may then resort to 'teacher baiting', causing the teacher to criticise still more! By making positive comments at the beginning of a lesson, the teacher is helping to pre-empt misbehaviour before it has a chance to build up. This strategy also encourages the children to believe that the teacher is taking a personal interest in them, and so helps to create a positive climate from the start.

A useful approach is to begin lessons by looking around the room, making positive comments on the behaviour of work of a number of individuals. The remarks could be directed towards those who are getting on with a curriculum activity, or those whose work has just been marked and which deserves approving comment, or those whom the teacher has seen behaving considerately round the school or in the playground, or those of whom positive things have been heard from other teachers or dinner ladies. Then, at intervals as the lesson proceeds, time should be found to look and move around the room, finding reasons for saying something about the work and behaviour of more pupils. The objective should be to include as many different pupils as possible during the course of a session.

A useful tactic is to ensure that early praise remarks include children who are complying with a specific target behaviour which has earlier been drawn to their attention. It may be that many children have been ignoring a particular classroom rule, or that too many incidents of inconsiderate behaviour have been evident, or that too many children have taken to wandering round the room unnecessarily. Praising examples of good behaviour with precise objectives in mind is a way of dealing positively with matters of current concern. It is, of course, important to be especially vigilant for children who display problem behaviour, though overdwelling on these pupils can paradoxically signal low expectations as well as cause resentment amongst the more conformist members of the class. It is therefore also important to acknowledge the good behaviour of typically well-behaved children.

(4) *Avoid actions which could spoil the effects of praise*

Teachers sometimes nullify the effects of praise by mixing negative comments with their approval or by criticising a child soon after praising. A reprimand can easily turn a positive atmosphere created by praise into a negative one. The effects of praise can also be impaired by the teacher's body language. Betraying surprise at good behaviour through facial expression is one example. Another is approving the behaviour of a child who is often troublesome, and then giving a sigh of exasperation when the child starts to misbehave again.

At the same time, simply ignoring misbehaviour will not make it go away. Even if the teacher manages to pay no attention, the other children will be less well-controlled and supply the attention which the offender is seeking. Ignoring misbehaviour must therefore always go hand in hand with finding favourable things to say. This is not easy with a child who tends to misbehave regularly. In this situation it often pays to praise a near-by child who is displaying the behaviour wanted. Where possible, it is effective to choose a pupil with whom the offender can identify, that is one whose behaviour is often quite similar to the offender's or one whom you know the offender admires. In these circumstances, the desired behaviour is more likely to be imitated. This action should then be followed by praising the child who has been disruptive as soon as there are signs of improvement, thus reinforcing the better behaviour.

(5) *Ensure that praise informs*

In a report on school behaviour, H. M. Inspectorate (1987) pointed out that praise needs to be specific if the pupil is to *learn* from it:

> The test question to be used in all praise should be: does it identify and

instance the nature of the satisfactory behaviour . . . The idea of what is satisfactory in school behaviour and achievement is not automatically learned or maintained but needs to be taught and supported. (para. 38)

It is thus important to try to say something which *provides positive feedback information* and to avoid vague remarks such as 'This is good work' or 'You're behaving well today'. Praise needs to be a response to something in particular which children have accomplished or are trying their best to do.

The evidence suggests that giving praise in a general way is no more effective than giving no praise at all (Kanouse *et al.*, 1981). What makes all the difference is the teacher describing, in her praise remarks, exactly what it is that justifies a favourable comment. An example might be 'Well done, Mary! You have remembered the rule about working quietly so as not to disturb others', or 'Trevor, that was good the way you helped David with his sums'. The same principle applies to remarks about academic achievement and written comments in children's work. Just putting a tick and 'Good' at the bottom of a piece of writing does not reinforce any particular aspect of the child's writing style because it does not say what it is about the work that warrants praise.

With older primary children, although praise is usually still welcome, a high quality of interaction and work feedback is usually of greater importance than praise as such. For those in the upper junior classes, the teacher's non-verbal feedback such as smiles and nods, along with constructive comment and challenging questions, is often more motivating than praise. The children then feel that the teacher is taking their progress seriously and setting high expectations. An example might be: 'That was a good answer, Pat. [Smile and maintain eye contact.] Now, I wonder if you have thought of something else. Just suppose . . . '. There is no need to fight shy of criticising children's work provided the feedback is essentially positive and useful. Praise used sparingly with constructive criticism (as distinct from fault-finding remarks) is more valuable and effective than abundant praise which lacks substance.

(6) *Praise for effort and for social acts as well as academic achievement*

The things children get praised for communicate messages about what teachers regard as important in life. Praise which dwells only on the best work in the National Curriculum foundation subjects, for instance, is divisive since it excludes many children by reducing the scope for praise. It is important to recognise those children who have tried hard and done their best. Equally it is important to reinforce good conduct and considerate behaviour as well as good work.

(7) *Use praise to communicate the message 'I know you can do it'*

In the infant stages, children seem to believe that any statement of public praise directed at a pupil is an indication of that child's ability (Nicholls, 1983). But after the age of 8 or 9, children become more sophisticated in their interpretations of praise. Giving older juniors praise for easy tasks or mediocre effort, for instance, can be construed as a sign of low ability, particularly if the teacher seems to be giving praise just for encouragement (Barker and Graham, 1987).

Teachers can modify children's beliefs about their potential through the way they phrase praise remarks. Children who experience learning or behaviour difficulties need to be assured that their efforts are worth while and that success is within their grasp. For example, they could be encouraged by the teacher saying, 'I can see that you've tried very hard, Gail. You're really getting the hang of fractions now', or 'I'm very pleased with you, Mark. That's the third day running when you have got on with your work quietly without disturbing Jason'.

Chapter 6 contains more detailed discussion of the effects of praise on children's self-perceptions.

(8) *Relay favourable remarks*

We like it when others pass on nice remarks about ourselves, and it is important to seize opportunities to do this in school. Teachers sometimes pass on to the pupils their personal frustrations with other members of staff by saying something like 'I'm getting sick and tired of hearing how rude you all are to Miss Octave in singing'. Sometimes, of course, a negative remark does need to be passed on, but it helps to reinforce considerate behaviour, and also encourage positive self-esteem, if the teacher relays a favourable remark about an individual who had clearly made a special effort: 'Melanie, Miss Smile has been telling me how polite you were when showing a visitor round this morning', or 'Derek, Mr Care says you were so helpful when Louise fell over in the playground'.

(9) *Be genuine*

Praise must be seen to be deserved. Older children are particularly sensitive about this. Praising just for encouragement will be devalued, at any rate above the infant stage, so it is important to look for something which properly merits a favourable comment.

(10) *For older pupils, consider whether the praise should be made in private rather than in public*

Children at any age, but more so as they get older, vary in their response to praise, which is perhaps partly why teachers often hold reservations about its efficacy. This points to the importance of noticing how individuals react to praise. Whereas infants usually enjoy being praised in front of the class or in assembly, some older primary children are self-conscious on these occasions. Teachers need to be sensitive to this possiblity, and consider whether a quiet expression of approval or thanks might be preferable to a public announcement.

Self-monitoring charts and behavioural programmes

A more sophisticated use of praise, often combined with rewards, is the central feature of management strategies based upon behavioural psychology. These rest on the assumption that behaviour is learned and maintained through reinforcement, and that behaviour which is not reinforced will disappear or be 'unlearned'. Dwelling upon underlying temperamental traits, the unconscious and other possible causative factors which cannot be directly observed is said to be unhelpful. Instead, behaviourists recommend planned intervention to change the circumstances which trigger off the unwanted behaviour, and giving praise and rewards for progress towards the desired behaviour.

The process of behavioural management begins with defining the behaviour and identifying the events surrounding it. This analysis is sometimes referred to as ABC (e.g. Wheldall and Glynn, 1989). The sequence can be represented as follows:

Antecedents → Behaviour → Consequences

'B' stands for the observed behaviour. This must be described objectively and precisely, such as 'shouting to another pupil' or 'running round the classroom' and not in vague or emotive terms like 'for ever being a nuisance'. 'A' stands for the antecedents of the behaviour. These are the events which occur immediately beforehand, or aspects of the physical and social environment in which the behaviour occurs, which could be stimulating the behaviour. In the last chapter, for instance, we discussed how misbehaviour could arise in classrooms through difficult access to materials, or particular seating arrangements, or the absence of instructions about what to do when a task is finished. 'C' stands for the consequences of the behaviour which may be encouraging the child to repeat the unwanted behaviour. For instance, a teacher might respond to a child saying rude words by getting angry and shouting at the child, or other children might laugh. Such actions could unwittingly help to maintain the unwanted behaviour since the child enjoys attracting the attention.

To change a child's behaviour by behavioural intervention involves changing the nature of the antecedents or the consequences or both. Changing the antecedents would therefore involve changing any aspects of the setting which appear to be contributing to the unwanted behaviour. Most of the suggestions made in the last chapter about forestalling behaviour problems are about antecedents. For instance, a child who gets restless and distracts others during individual work sessions might behave more acceptably if given more interesting or more carefully graded and shorter tasks; or placed in a less distracting part of the room; or seated by another child or nearer the teacher; or asked to do the kind of work involved at a different time during the day; or provided with more readily accessible materials.

Most behavioural experiments have emphasised the 'C' of the ABC approach through promoting wanted behaviour by making it more manageable and rewarding. Typically, this involves an intervention programme specially prepared for a pupil for whom regular positive feedback and changing antecedents are insufficient. It is important that the programme makes realistic demands on the child and concentrates on a single or small number of 'good behaviours' that the teacher wishes to reinforce.

One technique entails the use of a chart by which the child and teacher together identify target behaviours and monitor progress. The teacher begins by discussing the problem with the child and agreeing to focus on one particular target at a time. The statement should be worded simply and precisely and point to the behaviour wanted rather than not wanted: e.g. 'I will try to stay in my seat working quietly' rather than 'I won't run around the room', or 'I'll raise my hand when I want to say something or move', rather than 'I won't shout out'.

A tailor-made pictorial chart is then drawn depicting a favoured

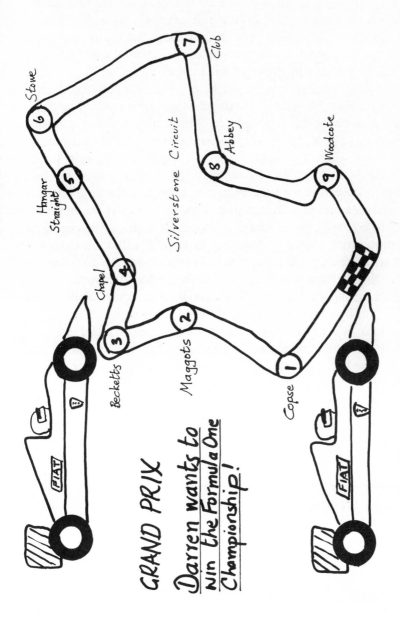

Figure 4.1   Example of a tailor-made self-monitoring behaviour chart

interest or pastime. This captures the child's imagination and promotes self-esteem by showing respect for the child's individuality. Embedded in the illustration are a number of circles or squares, as shown in the racing circuit example (figure 4.1). For a child who liked animals, the chart could display a tour round a zoo, for another who was keen on football it might depict the progress of a kicked ball as it travels through the air from player to goal.

An arrangement is then made whereby the child colours the chart to record progress towards the defined target behaviour. For this, the child or teacher makes a booklet (which the child could illustrate) containing pages of squares representing intervals of time over the part of the day when the programme is to operate. To begin with, the intervals should be short, say, ten minutes (or less). A tick is placed in a square at the end of the time interval to show that the target behaviour has been maintained. Although it helps if a support teacher is in the room to help with the monitoring, especially with very young children, self-monitoring should be encouraged where feasible as a sign of trust. In that case the teacher maintains light supervision, reinforcing honest recordings through praise. The agreement is that after so many ticks in the monitoring booklet, the child colours in a section of the pictorial chart, thus keeping a visual record of the progress made. As improved behaviour is demonstrated, the time intervals in the monitoring booklet can be extended and the chart gradually phased out. The chart system can be adapted to suit particular purposes, including the promotion of more acceptable behaviour outside the classroom, for example in the lunchroom and playground.

The child's active participation in determining the target behaviours, helping to make the materials, monitoring progress and filling in the chart often constitute sufficient reward, but some children may need a special incentive. Possible rewards for a completed chart include engagement in a favoured activity for part of an afternoon, a certificate for good behaviour from the head, or a letter of congratulations for the child to take home with the chart.

In cases of persistent problem behaviour, it can be beneficial if parents are involved more directly, as in a scheme in West Norfolk developed for children who are referred to the Behaviour Support Service. Here, the class teacher and a worker from the service sit down with the parent(s) to discuss the situation in a non-judgemental atmosphere. The parents are then invited to enter into an agreement whereby the child's favourite activities in the home – perhaps watching television, going on an outing – are varied according to weekly scores based on self-monitoring charts of the type shown in figure 4.1. Weekly contact with the parent is also maintained. As behaviour improves, the scheme is gradually phased out by extending the time by which behaviour targets are to be achieved. In this way the school and parents work together in developing a positive approach to the behaviour problem.

The next example of behavioural management is more time-consuming for the teacher and requires closer supervision, but it shows how a positive approach can be taken to help a child about whose behaviour many teachers would throw up their hands and say, 'There's simply nothing you can do'.

John, whose case has been described by his class teacher, Liz Saunders (1989), is a seven-year-old boy whom teachers had described as hyperactive, disruptive, attention-seeking and lacking in concentration. Investigation showed him to be working at the appropriate level for his needs, though he was frequently absent from school and the only task he really enjoyed was reading to the teacher. His mother, an alcoholic, expressed little interest in her son and the father did not live at home.

Detailed observations in the classroom by an educational psychologist had shown that John frequently failed to respond to simple requests such as putting his tray away. He constantly annoyed and teased other children, with whom he would not work, hitting them and taking their books. On the few occasions when he was in his seat he banged a pencil or ruler and made silly noises. He avoided getting down to work by saying he had first to find a pencil sharpener or a rubber or go to the toilet or have a drink.

In view of John's typical off-task behaviour, the teacher decided to try and increase his on-task behaviour. For John this was defined as sitting correctly in his chair with a pencil in his hand, his book open at the right place, working most of the time, and not interrupting other children. Going to the teacher to have his work checked was also accepted as being on-task.

The teacher made discreet observation for fifteen minutes each day for ten days while the class was engaged in formal individual work. She would look at John once a minute, and record on a tally chart whether or not the behaviour was on-task. To assess the accuracy of these assessments, another teacher observed John for one session and substantially agreed with the class teacher's recordings, which were therefore assumed to be valid. Over the ten-day period, it was noted that John was on-task 46 out of the 150 times he was observed. This provided base-line data by which the subsequent behavioural intervention could be evaluated.

During the intervention period, the teacher gave John high praise whenever she noticed he was on-task, as defined above, ignoring other behaviour unless his own or others' safety was in question. In order that the rest of the class would accept the teacher's specially favourable treatment of John and not try to distract him from work, it was agreed that every child could earn a token at the end of each day for trying hard, and another token if the task was especially well done. On Friday afternoons the children could exchange their tokens for one of thirteen activities. For each of these a popularity rating had been assigned based on the results of a class survey. Children who earned the most tokens could trade these in for the more favoured activities. For instance, one token would be sufficient for drawing or colouring, but five were necessary for operating a computer game.

Meanwhile, the teacher was keeping another tally chart of John's behaviour. After ten days, on-task behaviour had been recorded 104 times over 150 observations, showing a marked improvement from the base-line level. Also, for the first time, John was sufficiently motivated to finish his tasks, sometimes earning enough tokens to play a computer game on Friday afternoons. It was then decided to continue the programme for a futher period before phasing it out. The teacher very gradually reduced the incidence of praise and discontinued the token system, to which the class had responded most favourably.

Although, at the time of writing, the long-term results of the intervention are not known, the experiment is interesting for a number of reasons.

First of all, it shows that the behaviour of a child whom many might assume to be virtually beyond control can be changed for the better by means of positive intervention strategies within the classroom. Secondly, the case illustrates some central features of behavioural management. The teacher pin-pointed exactly what the undesirable behaviour consisted of and what was to count as desirable behaviour. She measured success by comparing records of careful observations before and during the intervention period. She used praise and rewards (based on what the children said they enjoyed doing) contingently and consistently to reinforce good behaviour, whilst ignoring most infringements. The phasing out of the intervention programme was carefully controlled.

Thirdly, the study shows how an intervention programme designed to improve the behaviour of one child can involve the whole class, whose interest in gaining a reward acts as an additional positive reinforcement of the target child's on-task behaviour. Indeed some teachers have successfully used behavioural intervention for a generally disruptive class without focussing on any particular individual. The activity rewards in the above experiment could serve this purpose. Examples of whole-class intervention can be found in Merrett (1985).

Judging from a recent survey (Coxhead and Gupta, 1989) many teachers resist the kind of methods described above. One obvious issue concerns the demands made on the busy teacher's time to keep accurate records and supervise the programme. On the other hand, the effort seems worthwhile when the child improves and is happier, when the rest of class do not suffer from the misbehaviour, and when less energy has to be spent reprimanding and dealing with complaints from the parents of other children.

More fundamentally, some teachers express misgivings about using what they regard as a mechanistic approach. The jargon often used in behavioural psychology, such as referring to children as 'subjects' whose behaviour is to be 'shaped', gives credence to this view. Many of the leading advocates of behavioural methods today, however, emphasise the importance of negotiating the intervention programme with the child. The original term 'behaviour modification', which might have a more natural home in the world of robots, is now used much less. The more recent term 'behaviour *management*' puts the emphasis on a cooperative approach. As Cheeseman and Watts (1985) put it, 'The pupil becomes a partner in the process, helping to decide on both the direction of change and the method used to bring it about. It is essential that the behaviour change is seen as a partnership' (p. 6). Hence it is important for the teacher to talk with the child about the purpose and nature of the intervention.

Another issue which worries some teachers is the emphasis given to extrinsic rewards rather than to intrinsic motivational factors. An important purpose of a school is to help children develop and deepen interests in activities for their own sake, so that motivation to work and behave well comes from within. In behavioural management, however, the use of rewards might suggest that the children are being encouraged to work and behave for reasons which originate outside themselves. They may even attribute any success to the prospect of a reward rather than to their personal agency.

It must be remembered, however, that the use of reprimand is also subject to this criticism since the children may work and behave simply to avoid the teacher's disapproval or anger rather than because they find the task inherently interesting. Nonetheless, it is important to examine the evidence about the consequences of tangible rewards. Most of it derives from the work of Mark Lepper and his associates in the United States. In the original investigation (Lepper *et al*. 1973), children who had demonstrated that they enjoyed drawing for its own sake, and who were then put in situations where they could expect a reward for drawing, tended to lose interest in the activity. The findings of numerous subsequent experiments, involving children of different ages and completing different kinds of tasks, have also tended to suggest that presenting children with extrinsic incentives may have adverse effects on later interest (Lepper, 1983).

It is obviously sensible to avoid giving rewards for good behaviour during activities which the child enjoys, even if unwanted behaviour sometimes occurs on these occasions. Even so, the more recent research suggests that the prospect of rewards is not necessarily harmful to intrinsic interest. What matters are the *conditions* in which rewards are offered so that the experience is a genuinely *educational* one.

First of all, it is important to help the child believe that he or she was responsible for the improvement. This means that the teacher must be careful not to give the impression that classroom work should be undertaken simply for the sake of a reward. Repetitively urging the child on with statements like 'If you want to play that computer game, you'll have to behave well' should therefore be avoided. Instead, once the child begins to improve, the teacher should use the opportunity to express interest in the work produced and to give plenty of feedback (Boggiano *et al*. 1982). By increasingly focussing attention on the work and decreasing references to the prospect of a reward, the teacher encourages the child to attribute success to personal ability and competence, and this in turn will help to develop the child's interest in the activity.

Secondly, the teacher should avoid giving the child work which consists only of getting 'right' answers. In those circumstances the child may resort to guessing the solution without bothering to test whether it makes sense, operating according to what Condry and Chambers (1979) call the 'manimax' principle: 'Learners are motivated to maximise reward with minimum effort'. Lepper and Green (1978) have shown that it is activities which involve problem-solving which are the most likely to engage the learner's interest and offer opportunities for the teacher to talk about the pupil's ideas and suggestions. Then, as the external rewards are phased out, the intrinsic interest of the activity continues to act as a source of motivation.

Thirdly, it seems that intrinsic interest will *increase* if the reward is contingent not just on mere task-engagement but on specified levels of performance (Boggiano and Ruble, 1979). The teacher may wish to focus on task-engagement as a first step. But as soon as possible she should make the reward dependent upon the achievement of certain standards. This again relates to the issue of perceived personal competence.

Lastly, it is important to consider the nature of the reward. Material rewards such as stars and smiley faces have no educational value in themselves, but if they are linked to certain activity rewards such as extra time for painting or using a computer, then worth-while pursuits are encouraged. Being commended by the head teacher or a letter to the parent are also educationally as well as psychologically useful since these have the potential to encourage talk about the activity in which the child has been engaged.

In short, the fact that an indiscriminate use of rewards can undermine subsequent intrinsic interest in some circumstances is no reason for not using rewards under certain conditions. These include drawing the children's attention to the good consequences of their efforts, ensuring that activities include problem-solving types of task, emphasising the importance of achieving certain standards as well as simple engagement in the task, and using rewards which are themselves educationally productive.

Chapter 5

Correcting Misbehaviour

Punitive regimes seem to be associated with worse rather than better standards of behaviour. This does not mean that punishments are not necessary ... [but that] schools need to establish a healthy balance between punishments and rewards.

Elton Report, p. 99

Compared with the strategies discussed in other chapters, reprimand and punishment would seem to represent a negative approach to classroom management. They sometimes suppress unacceptable behaviour and deter others from misbehaving; but they can also exacerbate behaviour problems and alienate children from schooling, inducing anxiety and feelings of rejection, even encouraging truancy. A reprimanding style of classroom management can also reinforce attention-seeking behaviour by giving it public status. Regular outbursts of anger and unreasonable punishment expose all pupils, the innocent as well as the guilty, to inappropriate adult models. The aggression may then be imitated and displaced, leading to bullying and harassment.

The possible adverse effects of reprimand and punishment certainly suggest that they should never be used as principal management strategies. However, the fact that there are dangers in their misuse and over-use does not mean that they have no constructive role to play in school. Apart from their deterrent potential, they have the propensity to make a contribution to children's social development by emphasising the boundaries of tolerable behaviour. As with praise and rewards, they can be used both counterproductively and productively, their effectiveness depending on the observance of certain conditions.

Reprimands

Given the need to reprimand and punish on occasions, how can these measures be used to best effect?

(1) *Use reprimands sparingly*

The Junior School Project demonstrated that teachers who are constantly criticising are the least successful in managing classroom behaviour. Conversely, those who are firm but also focus on good behaviour are the most successful (Mortimore *et al.* 1988). This suggests that reprimand should be used with discrimination and not allowed to characterise the teacher's management style. Its use will then have greater impact.

Because reprimanding often brings about the desired response in a classroom, at least in the short term, its use can be rewarding for the teacher. This being so, it is easy for classroom relationships to deteriorate as the teacher slides into the habit of scolding and being critical. Children who normally enjoy positive feedback and receive recognition for their good work and behaviour do not usually want to upset the teacher, and in this situation non-verbal reprimanding – frowning, pausing for silence, a surprised facial expression – or mild verbal correction is often sufficient. Talking to the child after class will also be more effective and educative when reprimanding is discriminating and relationships are generally sound.

For small misdemeanours, reprimanding can sometimes be avoided by making positive statements. Take the common command 'Stop mucking around and get on with your work!'. This is often ineffective because (a) it imputes bad motives, (b) it reinforces the unwanted behaviour by giving it public status, and (c) it signals unreasonably that the teacher's support is conditional upon the pupil's improved behaviour. A statement such as 'Sandra, I see you have a problem – I'll come over and help you in a minute' should be more effective since it is positive and supportive, indicating the teacher's recognition that the unwanted behaviour may be arising from a work problem.

(2) *Reprimand firmly but quietly*

The manner of reprimanding is equally important. Shouting or maintaining a loud voice in order to control children is unproductive and stressful. In one study of classroom behaviour (O'Leary and

O'Leary, 1970), some teachers were asked to reprimand softly, going up to offenders so that only they could hear. Behaviour in the class-room improved. The teachers were then asked to return to their customary loud reprimands. The behaviour worsened. The research-ers concluded that ideally teachers should use soft reprimands most of the time. Occasional loud reprimands, if needed, will then be all the more effective.

Reprimanding by shouting is unprofessional for a number of reasons. One is that it disrupts the work of the class and induces an unsettled atmosphere. Another is that it sets an example for the very kind of behaviour which is not wanted, the teacher effectively teaching children to shout when things don't go their way. Thirdly, loud reprimands encourage disrupting behaviour in those children who yearn for more adult attention but find difficulty in gaining it by socially acceptable means. They find that playing up in class pays off in making the teacher take notice of them, but of course it is not the kind of notice that responds satisfactorily to their basic needs. Fourthly, loud reprimands may provide entertainment for some children who enjoy the spectacle of a teacher getting angry and upset. This not only makes it difficult for the teacher to gain respect: it also helps to maintain the unwanted behaviour. For being bad is being somebody.

Lastly, but importantly, reprimanding by shouting is bad practice because the loudness of the teacher's voice prevents the offender from thinking clearly and attending to the message which the reprimand is meant to convey. With young, less-able and anxious children in particular, the teacher's shouting simply makes the culprit confused and upset, and is therefore of no educative value and of doubtful use as a deterrent.

Rather than shout across the room, it is more effective to move towards the pupil, quietly name him or her, and, softly but firmly deliver the reprimand. At the same time, it is important to be positive by pointing out the behaviour which is wanted, and then re-directing the child's attention to some feature of the work activity.

(3) *Make clear that it is the behaviour which is unacceptable, not the child*

Another important condition for effective reprimanding is that the teacher focuses on the act, not on personality factors. This means that she should refrain from directing attention to her own power or from suggesting that the child is inherently naughty. Teachers who reprimand with authoritarian remarks like 'You will do as you're told', or 'I am not putting up with that kind of behaviour' make the criticism a personal matter. Hostile or sarcastic comments such as 'Why is it that it's always John I have to speak to?' suggest that the child is irreedemably naughty. The effect is to create feelings of alienation and set up expectations that John will always be a nuisance. Through her manner of reprimanding, the teacher needs to convey the idea that it is the behaviour which is unacceptable, not the child. It may help to get over the fact that the reprimand is justified by saying something like 'That was a thoughtless thing to do', but not 'You're a thoughtless person'.

It is often appropriate to point out to children that misbehaving could have adverse consequences for their progress, for example 'George, I'm sure you don't want to get behind'. For inconsiderate behaviour, it could be useful to say something like 'Jennifer, I know you wouldn't like it if someone did that to you'. This draws attention to the unpleasant effects of the child's behaviour without suggesting that the child has an unpleasant personality. Skilful teachers sometimes manage to express surprise whilst reprimanding. This helps the culprit to believe that the teacher does not view the behaviour as a symptom of general naughtiness. The child's sense of personal worth is thus preserved. In some circumstances, it may be necessary to specify a punishment which will follow the next offence. Children do respect teachers who are prepared to punish, provided it is not habitual and the sanction is perceived as reasonable and deserved.

(4) *Reprimand before the misbehaviour escalates*

The timing of a reprimand affects its impact. Telling a child off when the unacceptable behaviour has been allowed to build up may make the child feel guilty but will not have the same inhibitory effect as a reprimand which nips the bad conduct in the bud (Aronfreed, 1976). If the misbehaviour is minor but repetitive, it is often effective to ignore it at first and to keep an eye open in case of further trouble. In that event, the reprimand will have greater impact if delivered as the child *starts* to misbehave again since it will then be associated in the child's mind with the *temptation* to misbehave rather than with the enjoyment of misbehaving.

Punishment

Some of the points made about reprimand, such as being sparing in its use and focussing on the reprehensibility of the act and not of the child, apply equally to punishment. Again, the timing is important: the longer it is after the event, the more difficult it is for young children to link the punishment to the offence.

Punishment in school, however, raises further issues which require the teacher to make sensitive professional judgements. When reprimanding, it is easier to appeal to the child's understanding, but the potentially educative role of punishment is less apparent. It is also harder to make amends for an unjustly severe punishment, or for punishing the wrong child, than for reprimanding a child too harshly or unfairly.

For punishment to seem fair, it must operate against a background of rules and expectations which the children know and generally respect. Punishing children should be reserved for repeated offences, and should not be given if it is apparent that the child is trying to improve, however slow the progress may be. The offender should first be given a clear warning in a firm, matter-of-fact way. Once the teacher has issued a warning, it is important to follow it up at the first infringement, or her authority will not be respected.

It is often said that teachers should be consistent in their use of punishment. Certainly punishment will not suppress unwanted behaviour if used in an arbitrary fashion, for children will then find it difficult to form a clear concept of what counts as acceptable and unacceptable conduct. On the other hand, the inflexible use of punishment which takes no account of circumstances could be regarded as unfair. For punishment to be respected and effective, it is important that both the offender and the rest of the class perceive it as deserved.

Here, however, the teacher is faced with a dilemma, for what an adult may regard as fair and just a child may not. According to Piaget (1932), children in their early years of schooling will not generally have the maturity to understand the justice of varying punishment according to the circumstances, such as whether the act was accidental, intentional or well-motivated, because they focus on the deed itself. A large but accidental misdeed is thus worse than a small but deliberate one. This characteristic of young children, which Piaget called 'moral realism', means that teachers who punish one child but not another for the same offence could be greeted by the cry 'It's not fair, Miss!', even though the circumstances were different.

There is no easy answer to this problem, but a number of points can be made. First of all, Piaget's evidence about young children's immature moral awareness has been largely superseded by the evidence of later better-constructed studies. The more recent research suggests that by the age of six or seven most children realise that blame and punishment is more or less deserved according to the perpetrator's intentions and motives *provided that* the situation is simply presented (Fincham, 1983). While older children are certainly more discriminating in their judgements, the younger ones can and do take some account of circumstances. Indeed, as experienced teachers and parents can testify, young children often plead 'Yes, but I didn't mean it', or even 'Yes, but he made me do it' or 'Yes, but I was only trying to help'. Most primary school children from quite an early age, then, are capable of understanding that, say, Sharon should be punished for splashing paint on Tracy because she didn't like her, whereas Trevor should not be punished for splashing paint on David when his hand slipped – but the younger the child, the more teachers need to explain the different situations carefully and patiently. Indeed, this is part of their job as educators.

Secondly, the ability to make discriminating judgements about behaviour is not something that just happens as a result of growing up. It is very much dependent on the way we are treated during the course of our childhood by the significant adults in our lives. Maturity in making moral judgements develops earlier in young children who live in an environment where adults refrain from being bossy and domineering and appeal to the child's developing sense of reasoning about what is right and wrong (Kohlberg, 1968). We also know that children who experience a warm, compassionate un-punitive style of upbringing will learn earlier to empathise with other people's point of view (Hoffman, 1970; Light, 1979). All this has implications for the teacher's style of classroom management as well as for parental practices. In particular the teacher's manner should convey the message that when children are reprimanded or punished it is not *just because* they have been disobedient or frustrated the teacher (which would reinforce the young child's dependence on adult authority) but because they have disregarded the feelings and needs of others.

A third point which needs to be made here is that we often need to respond to the behaviour of children *as if* they were more mature than in fact they are. It is part of a teacher's job to help children gradually view themselves as responsible moral agents who, as such, deserve to be blamed for thoughtless or mean acts. Experiencing the unpleasant-

66

ness of punishment from an adult with whom relationships are fundamentally good has an educative function in helping children to develop the feelings associated with 'being responsible' and therefore subject to blame. This does not, of course, justify any sort of punishment or its regular use. But it does point to the possibility that moderate punishment, used sparingly when other methods have been tried, has a part to play in helping children to feel accountable for what they do. *Evaluation of consequences of behav.*

Encourage wherever possible, not just when punishments or reprimands

Types of punishment

Punishment, to be punishment, must be unpleasant for the offender. But some forms of unpleasantness are ruled out on the grounds that they are either ineffective or fail to treat children as persons. It would therefore be unprofessional, as well as unethical, to demean children through sarcasm, or to apply derogatory labels to them.

Most punishments are problematic in one way or another. This is why it is so important for teachers not to rely on them, but to ensure that it is the more positive approaches (such as those discussed in other chapters) that characterise their teaching and management styles. However, given that punishment is necessary from time to time, it is important to choose the kind which has greatest chance of helping the child to behave better without the unfortunate side-effects listed at the start of this chapter. In deciding what measure to take, new teachers will also need to take account of the customary practices in the school.

Punishments fall into two broad categories: those which deprive offenders of some aspect of their freedom and those which inflict unpleasantness directly.

(A) *Punishing by depriving the child of freedom*

(1) LOSING PRIVILEGES OR FREE TIME
Children who misbehave in school are sometimes deprived of participating in a favoured activity. The idea is to prompt offenders to reflect whether the illegitimate enjoyment derived from misbehaving is worth the cost of losing opportunities which can be legitimately enjoyed. The technique is therefore technically called 'response cost'. Of course, the activity lost must not be part of the formal curriculum, to which all children - including those misbehaving - are entitled. Teachers should therefore refrain from, say, depriving a child of a swimming or games lesson.

A problem here is that unless the activity is really enjoyable, having to miss it will not be a punishment. Yet if the activity is one to which the child is especially looking forward to, perhaps a class outing, the child may simply feel resentful and even try to shift the blame on to another pupil. In any case, by the time the event occurs the circumstances of the misdemeanour are past history. For maximum impact, a punishment should follow the offence without delay. Ideally, then, the privileges or freedoms lost should be those which would otherwise be enjoyed the same day. Losing the next playtime, or part of it, is often quite effective for this reason.

Detaining children after school is fraught with difficulties, especially in the case of young children who need to be accompanied home. Local Education Authorities and school governors may have guidelines about the use of detention, and these should be given in the school prospectus. Parents must always be given adequate notice, and teachers who do not do this can be accused of false imprisonment! Because it is therefore difficult to arrange for detention after school on the same day as the offence, the punishment is often less effective than alternative, more immediate measures.

Teachers should refrain from keeping in the whole class. Piaget's (1932) main conclusion on punishment of whole groups still holds good: that even very young children regard it to be unfair since the innocent members of the class are as inconvenienced as the guilty.

(2) SEGREGATING THE PUPIL

Teachers sometimes segregate misbehaving children by making them sit alone away from friends, perhaps facing a wall. The social embarrassment which this causes may be an effective deterrent both to the offender and to the class as a whole. The child is also no longer receiving attention from other children in the class who may be helping to maintain the problem behaviour. However, the punishment carries the risk of making the child feel unwanted and thus exacerbating the problem. It would be professionally irresponsible, therefore, to use this strategy in order to shelve responsibility for the child during the rest of the lesson. Rather the teacher should make clear that the offender can return to his or her seat after a specified short period of time (say, 5 minutes). When this time has elapsed, and provided the child has not continued to misbehave, the punishment should be stopped and the child asked to promise to behave acceptably. Opportunity should then be seized to praise for good behaviour or work, and so restore a positive relationship and reintegrate the child in the group.

In some schools, children who keep disturbing the rest of the class and making undue demands on the teacher's time are sent to another classroom, or are given work to do near the head's room, in the school office, or in another designated area. For this to count as a punishment, the child must not receive sympathetic attention from other staff or pupils. Of course, this again raises the risk of compounding the problem by making the child feel unwanted.

Asking children to stand outside the classroom is not good practice because the culprit may find the experience more enjoyable than classroom work, especially if friends can be attracted through the window!

Segregating children as a punishment should not be confused with management strategies which involve moving a child to another seat where the teacher can give support more easily, or arranging for the child to work with another teacher for a short period of time in a different environment. Since the child is now getting *more* attention, such measures do not constitute punishment but alternative teaching provision to meet the child's needs. Admittedly the borderline between 'support' and 'punishment' is a fuzzy one since in some circumstances the child may perceive the alternative teaching arrangements as a punitive measure, especially if ordered to accept them in a peremptory manner. Nonetheless, a judgement must be made about what is in the child's best interests, whether it is punishment because it is deserved, or whether more structured support is required to enable the child to succeed and behave acceptably more easily.

(B) *Direct punishments*

(1) A SEVERE TELLING-OFF
This is a punishment rather than just a reprimand since the intention is to inflict unpleasantness by shaming the child. As with ordinary reprimands, it is more effective if delivered privately. At best, it can get across the reprehensibility of the offence, but if the teacher shouts or makes demeaning remarks, the child may become resentful, as well as confused about the moral message which the punishment is intended to convey.

(2) DOING EXTRA TASKS

Teachers sometimes make children write out lines. The meaningless-
ness of the exercise may be why it is often laughed at rather than
respected. It is probably better to give offenders a socially useful task,
such as clearing up litter, tidying a cupboard, putting up a display,
sorting books in the library, putting out equipment for science, finding
missing articles. Of course there is a sense in which these impositions
are not punishments but opportunities for the child to feel socially
useful and build up a better rapport with the teacher. Extra written
work is usually best avoided since this may turn the child off the
curriculum area in question.

(3) SENDING THE CHILD TO THE HEAD TEACHER

This must be reserved for serious or repeated offences, otherwise the
class teacher is liable to lose her position of authority in the classroom
as well as her professional status in the eyes of the head and colleagues.
The nature of the behaviour for which this strategy is permitted, and
the procedure to be employed, should be clear and agreed by all the
staff.

(4) ENLISTING THE SUPPORT OF PARENTS

A letter may be written to the parents, or they may be asked to come up
to the school. Certainly parents need to be informed about their child's
misbehaviour before it becomes a serious problem, but if they regard
this as a punitive measure they may over-react and 'take it out' on the
child. It is therefore important to discuss positive management
strategies with parents, such as those used in some West Norfolk
primary schools, described in the last chapter (see p. 54–55). Other
constructive ways of involving parents are discussed in chapters 6 and 8.

In view of all these 'ifs' and 'buts' about different types of
punishment, what conclusions can be drawn? As we have seen, for
maximum effectiveness punishment should be administered without
delay and without humiliating the child. For moral reasons, it should
be sufficiently unpleasant to prompt the child to 'think again' and act
more responsibly, but not so unpleasant that the child perceives the
'punishment' as unjust and becomes alienated from the values which
the school is trying to reinforce. On these criteria, of the various
punishments discussed, losing a playtime or favoured extra-curricular

activity, giving the child extra tasks to do of the kind described earlier, or segregating the pupil for a short stipulated time interval, would seem to be the most appropriate measures.

Punishment and the law

The 1986 Education (No. 2) Act abolished all forms of corporal punishment in maintained schools and all special schools. The law applies to 'informal' corporal punishment such as slapping, throwing chalk and rough handling, as well as formal corporal punishment such as hitting with a ruler or caning. The only legal justification for the use of physical force against a child is that it was necessary to prevent damage or injury. Thus a teacher would be acting lawfully by pulling children away to break up a fight, but not if the offenders were then hit as a punishment.

The 1986 Act also set out requirements which must be observed in cases of exclusion from a maintained school. The precise procedures are set out in the Articles of Government for each school and should be summarised in the school prospectus. A child can be excluded from school only by the Head, who must decide whether the measure is temporary, indefinite or permanent. In most cases it will be temporary, and a date must be fixed for the pupil's return. When a pupil is excluded for more than five days altogether in any one term, the Head has a duty to explain the decision to the governors and the LEA. The Head must tell the parents about the nature of any exclusion, the reason for it, and how long it is to last. Parents must also be told of their rights of appeal to the governing body and LEA.

Managing confrontation

Children sometimes get up-tight when being told-off, answering back, going sulky, or refusing to comply with requests. Incidents most easily occur with older primary school children who have come to associate reprimand and punishment with rejection or hostility. Children who are depressed because of discord at home may appear to welcome or even seek the excitement of confrontation as a means of relieving their feelings of helplessness. Paradoxically, of course, the experience may contribute further to their state of anxiety.

Confrontation may also come about with children who have not learned the social skills of apologising or explaining circumstances to those in authority. The less articulate pupils may have difficulty in trying to explain extenuating circumstances without making it sound as if they are unwilling to accept the consequences of their actions. Children may also confront teachers as a way of compensating for poor attainment, for instance in reading.

There is also a greater risk of confrontation with teachers whom the children sense are perpetually on the look-out for trouble, and who seem to 'have it in' for certain individuals regarded as 'trouble-makers'. Equally at risk are teachers who reprimand or impose sanctions for incidents that they have not personally witnessed and before they have verified the identity of the culprit. This may arise when a commotion is heard in the classroom or a fight breaks out in the playground or one pupil comes to complain about another. In cases like this there is a real danger of creating a legitimate grievance through telling off or punishing the wrong child. The chances of such incidents are especially high when the teacher is preoccupied in helping an individual or group (or is taken up with children demanding her attention while on playground supervision) and fails to keep a roving eye.

However much a teacher may feel aggrieved by a child's behaviour, confrontation almost always damages relationships since it produces a situation in which neither teacher nor pupil is prepared to back down for fear of losing status. The best way to avoid confrontation is to create conditions in which it is least likely to occur. Hence it is important to use preventive and pro-active strategies, such as those discussed in the previous two chapters, and to avoid shouting at children, using sarcasm, physically prodding the pupil, or insisting on implicit obedience for its own sake.

The risk of confrontation is also reduced when the teacher refuses to make an issue out of the incident there and then. An example would be a child arriving late. There is less possibility of confrontation if the teacher settles the child down quickly and deals with the reason for lateness later in the lesson when the class is engaged in activities.

All the same, confrontations can arise even with experienced teachers. If a child does answer back or is rude or abusive, the general aim should be to deal with the situation without making matters worse and damaging prospects of building up a positive relationship with the pupil. It is important to try to set the class a model for dealing non-aggressively with threatening situations. This is not easy, but there are two temptations which are worth resisting.

The first is to lose your temper or bark back with a remark such as 'How dare you speak to me like that!', or to confirm that the remark has been taken as abusive by giving it or the child a label – 'I'm not going to stand here and put up with your rudeness'. An emphasis on power or status together with the imputation of bad motives might tempt the child to continue to wind the teacher up. The other temptation to resist is to interrupt the lesson by spending time dealing with the situation there and then in front of the class. This gives the child public status, which again could be rewarding, and may cause further problems for the teacher in having to regain class control.

It would obviously be wrong and ineffective to ignore abusive behaviour, so instead the confrontation has to be deflected and the incident discussed privately later on. One strategy is to say calmly, 'I want to talk to you after the lesson'. Both teacher and child then have time to get control of themselves. Later in the lesson it would be appropriate to give the child positive support and encouragement, and then, when the rest of the class is dismissed, to speak about the incident in a gently, non-threatening way. Since the child knows that the behaviour is unacceptable, making a scene about it will only confirm that you are angry or upset; so the strategy is not to get on your high horse but to make clear that you want to understand the problem.

In short, it is important for the whole class that the teacher presents a model of calm but purposeful behaviour in a confrontation whilst also showing the offender that she wants relationships to be friendly and constructive. If in the event it turns out that the child has a legitimate grievance, then the correct action to take is to apologise. This sets the right example and, in the long-term, should earn respect.

Chapter 6

Encouraging Positive Thinking

Good behaviour has a lot to do with pupils' motivation to learn.
Elton Report, p. 104

Among the common problems with which primary school teachers have to deal are children being 'off task' in various ways. This includes attempts to avoid work, being easily distracted and distracting others, and what the Elton Committee quaintly described as 'calculated idleness'. This chapter looks at a range of inter-related approaches to issues such as these which reflect problems of pupil motivation.

Communicating positive expectations

'Our evidence suggests that pupils tend to live up, or down, to teachers' expectations'. This statement from the Elton Report (p. 142) was based mainly on the Committee's own observations and, in the case of primary schools, the Junior School Project. The latter had shown that children behaved more responsibly when they were asked to accept responsibilities by managing their own work within clear guidelines, rather than being 'told' what to do all the time.

There is another body of research, mainly American, which shows the potency of teacher expectations in influencing the level of children's achievements and attitude to learning, and which has implications for classroom behaviour. The seminal work was published in a book called *Pygmalion in the Classroom* by Robert Rosenthal and Lenore Jacobson (1968). This purported to demonstrate that achievements in the early primary years were influenced by the expectations which teachers held about their pupils' potential for academic growth – a phenomenon which has come to be known as the 'Pygmalion effect'. Although the design of this study came in for a good deal of criticism, numerous recent studies have confirmed that teacher expectations do have effects on children's work and behaviour, at least by maintaining rather than narrowing differences in levels of motivation and achievement.

One of the most recent and interesting investigations was carried out by Karen Brattesani and her colleagues (1984) in classrooms of 7- to 12-year-olds in urban ethnically-mixed schools. The researchers tried to find answers to two questions: (1) Did pupils guage teachers' perceptions of them accurately? (2) Did differences in teachers' perceptions significantly affect the pupils' achievements? The inquiries were conducted by comparing pupils' perceptions and progress in classrooms of contrasting ethos: those in which the teachers showed marked differential treatment of high and low achievers, and those in which the teachers treated all children much the same regardless of their previous attainment. In the former, for example, teachers gave high-achieving children more opportunities to participate and more choice of activity.

In answer to the first question, it was found that pupils in the 'high differentiation' classes did interpret the teachers' differential treatment of high and low achievers in terms of different expectations about their capabilities, and that these perceptions were generally accurate. The answer to the second research question was equally clear. In classrooms where pupils perceived a wide range of teacher-expectations, the difference in progress between high and low achievers was significatly more pronounced. It seemed that in these classes pupils were responding to, and even exaggerating, the perceptions they believed their teachers had of them.

This research focussed largely on children's reading attainment. Given that there is a well-established close association between progress in reading and social behaviour (e.g. McGee *et al.*, 1984; Mortimore *et al.*, 1988), the conclusions of this study have clear implications for motivation and classroom discipline. To encourage good behaviour as well as academic progress, it is important to hold realistic but positive expectations of all pupils.

Let us look more closely at what some teachers do which betrays their expectations of pupils' learning potential. Research in primary classrooms by Fry (1987) and reviews by Brophy (1983) and Cooper and Tom (1984) suggest that some teachers interact more frequently and more supportively with pupils about whom they hold high expectations. They are more likely to smile, nod their heads, make eye-to-eye contact, and praise for right or unusual answers. They also criticise them less for wrong answers, stay with them longer when they have trouble answering a question, and show greater willingness to repeat or re-phrase questions and give clues. By contrast, with low-expectation pupils, these teachers are apt to give up more quickly before redirecting questions to more able children in the class, thus inadvertently making success more difficult. According to Fry (1987), teachers' positive communications are at a peak in January and thereafter decline, reaching a marked 'low' by the end of the spring term as their patience wears thin!

Of course, all teachers are bound to recognise that some pupils stand a greater chance of doing well than others, and much of the difference in their treatment of pupils is a perfectly appropriate response to accurate assessments of their differing learning needs. For example, teachers individualise work programmes on this basis. As Brophy (1983) remarks, 'A teachers's instruction of low achievers should be judged on the degree to which it meets their needs and maximises their achievement progress and not on its similarity to the teacher's treatment of high achievers' (p. 657). Nonetheless, from the evidence which Brophy and others have reviewed, it seems that *some* teachers – but not all – treat pupils as if they were more different than they actually are, and that these teachers tend more than others to maintain (if not to enhance) differences between them. By contrast, other and more effective teachers adopt a pro-active stance. They hold higher levels of expectancy about low-achievers and less well-behaved children, and they resist indulging in negative typing. In so far as they do treat pupils differently, they do so in order to enhance their learning opportunities.

Why it is that some teachers are more prone than others to communicate low expectations to their pupils? Cooper and Tom (1984) argue that teachers who are more restrictive in their interactions with low-achieving children seem to be afraid of losing class control. They are prepared to interact on friendly and supportive terms when these pupils are working alone, but they are nervous about the consequences of giving them too much freedom in class discussion. Fearful of unhelpful remarks, or just not knowing how to handle wrong or inappropriate answers, they call upon them less often, even ignoring them when their hands are up, and they criticise them more for misconduct or poor answers.

To some extent, then, the problem of teacher expectations is a problem about teachers' confidence concerning their teaching and management skills. Nonetheless, there are measures which all teachers can take to avoid the risks of generating self-fulfilling prophecies resulting from low levels of expectancy.

76

(1) *Avoid forming inaccurate expectations in the first place*

Cooper and Tom (1984) identify three particular sources of potentially unreliable information about pupils. One is the experience of teaching an older brother or sister. It is certainly wrong to assume that children within the same family are necessarily the same in temperament or motivation to learn. A second is remarks made by former teachers (which are often as much a function of the teachers as the pupil). A third source of possibly inaccurate expectations is social stereotypes based on race or culture.

There is also a danger of developing low expectations of some pupils as a result of reading their records from the previous year with another teacher. This does *not* mean that teachers should avoid keeping and reading pupils' records, but rather that they should be alert to the danger of forming and signalling low expectations as a result. It is important that school records help to communicate positive expectations to succeeding teachers by including notes of effective strategies that have been used with individuals who have presented learning or behaviour problems. Now that school records are open to parents, positive comment is also important to promote positive expectations among members of the child's family.

We are all human, and it is obviously impossible to avoid picking up unfair impressions of individual pupils. However, the risk of generating low expectations of learning and behavioural potential might be reduced if teachers are determined to look for evidence which refutes negative labels which pupils have acquired. Equally it is important to refrain from indulging in negative staffroom gossip about 'my problem children'.

(2) *Avoid overt comparisons of achievement between pupils and focus instead on individual progress*

The work of Mitman and Lash (1988) has suggested that seating children in the classroom by ability and comparing their levels of achievement in front of the class are two of the most important factors which may lead low-achieving pupils to exaggerate teachers' expectations of them. Given that effective teaching depends on some individualisation of work programmes, pupils are bound to make comparisons of each other's achievement levels. In giving feedback, however, the teacher can draw pupils' attention to progress relative to their past achievement, thus encouraging them to worry less about how they are doing compared with others. If rewards are given, they should not be competitive (which highlights differences between pupils) but based on individual progress and effort.

(3) *Avoid remarks or signals which could give the impression that pupils' learning difficulties are irremediable*

As we have seen, teachers can signal low expectations through verbal and non-verbal cues such as not calling on certain pupils, giving them too little time to answer, or hurredly re-directing a question to a more able pupil. This can unfairly imply that the learning problem lies with the child rather than the way in which the curriculum is organised and presented. It is therefore important to try to ask questions to which low achievers can realistically respond, to re-phrase questions to present the problem more helpfully, and to encourage effort through smiling, nodding, maintaining eye contact and praising for appropriate answers.

(4) *Set goals in terms of floors, not ceilings*

With pupils of whom low expectations are held, teachers sometimes set goals in terms of what is minimally acceptable rather than what is realistically achievable (Brophy, 1983). This gives the pupils the impression that they are not able to respond successfully to challenging tasks. Given that children try to make their performance match the teacher's level of expectancy, then by raising the level of expectancy children will raise their levels of learning. It is therefore important to set goals in terms of what the child's present progress suggests might be achievable rather than just what could pass as acceptable. The provision of activities which 'stretch' pupils should not be the privilege of more able children. Of course, the degree of challenge must be realistic for the individual pupil, as discussed below (p. 79–80).

(5) *Avoid labelling language*

Negative expectations are easily set up through phrases which teachers use in reprimanding. Examples are: 'Alan, I see that you are messing about as usual' and 'Why is it always Karen who keeps us waiting?' The use of terms such as 'problem pupils' when speaking to other members of staff or even to ourselves reinforces the belief that the pupil will not change and sets up a vicious circle of negative expectations (see Chapter 2). It is better to think and speak in terms of 'pupils with behaviour problems', which does not suggest that the source of difficulty is necessarily something internal to the children. The official term 'children with special needs' has the important advantage of pointing to professional responsibilities, though there is a tendency to slide into talking about 'SEN pupils'. This sounds uncomfortably like the outdated and labelling term 'ESN pupils' and draws attention to the pupil rather than the need. It is, to be sure, difficult to find satisfactory terms which reduce the risk of labelling, but perhaps it is worth being a little tortuous in our everyday conversations to avoid placing pupils into 'medical' categories. In short, we need to ensure that the vocabulary we use in discussion about problem behaviour is contributing to solving the problem, not to perpetuating it.

Enhancing self-esteem

One of the ways in which human beings vary in their self-perceptions is the extent to which each 'considers himself to be capable, significant, successful, worthy' (Coopersmith, 1967, p. 5). Those who have positive self-concepts are said to be high in self-esteem, and those with negative self-concepts are low in self-esteem. Self-esteem is thus about how we evaluate our own worth.

Research suggests an association between school behaviour, school achievement and levels of self-esteem, but it is not clear which is cause and which is effect in this triangular relationship. Very likely, the influences work in all directions, but it is generally accepted that low self-esteem leads to lack of confidence, anxiety, difficulty in making friends, difficulty in adjusting to school, low achievement and poor relationships with others (Kagan *et al.*, 1969).

The seminal work on self-esteem was conducted by Stanley Coopersmith (1967), who observed and interviewed over 1,700 10-year-old-boys. Coopersmith found that the level of self-esteem was associated with styles of upbringing. Boys high in self-esteem had parents who wanted to know their sons' opinions and valued what they had to say, making them feel that they mattered and were significant as persons. By contrast, those with a low self-esteem had parents who did not treat them seriously, who were inconsistent in the standards of behaviour demanded, and were either permissive or punitive in their control strategies.

However, it is now realised that, although relationships with parents are particularly important in the development of self-esteem, relationships with other significant adults also materially affect the image which children have of themselves. Through undue criticism, negative labelling and sarcasm, teachers can easily reinforce children's low self-esteem, though fortunately they can also enhance it through positive measures. Indeed the Junior School Project demonstrated that the school has a *greater* influence on the way children regard themselves than background factors. It would appear, therefore, that teachers play a significant part in encouraging pupils to think positively or negatively about their worth.

Self-esteem is clearly affected by many factors, but the following appear to be particularly important:

(1) having the opportunity to succeed;
(2) appreciating your own successes;
(3) believing that others value you; and
(4) having a strong sense of identity.

The ideas which follow are therefore grouped under these headings.

Having the opportunity to succeed

High self-esteem appears to be a consequence of successfully meeting challenges. This has a number of important implications for classroom motivation. First, as we saw in the last section, children not only need to be provided with challenging activities but also need to know that the teacher expects them to respond successfully. The message should be: 'This is hard, but I know you can do it' (Purkey, 1970). Secondly, however, the activities must be *realistically* challenging. Too much practice work will lead to boredom; equally, work which is too demanding will lead to frustration. Both these situations are unproductive educationally and may lead to disruptive behaviour. What therefore is needed is a challenge which is beyond the pupils' current levels of achievement but also within their grasp. It is to be hoped that, in spite of current concerns about negative backwash effects, experience in assessing children's work in the National Curriculum will help teachers to develop the necessary diagnostic skills by which they can suitably 'match' tasks to individuals' achievement levels.

Thirdly, children will be motivated by challenges which they enjoy. It is therefore important to present a variety of activities which cater for the range of interests and skills among pupils. Schools clubs and other extra-curricular activities increase the opportunities for children to show what they can do and to develop new skills and interests.

Fourthly, children will be motivated by challenges if they know that support is available when they are experiencing difficulty. Setting aside time to talk to the class and individuals about what they have done is a crucial element in classroom management strategy. It provides reassurance for the pupils and signals to the teacher the kind of provision which then needs to be made.

Fifthly, children will be motivated by challenges if success can be experienced early and regularly. Nothing succeeds like success! This is why it is important to present complicated activities, such as learning new concepts in mathematics, as a series of short-term manageable goals which facilitate positive and frequent feedback.

Lastly, from research studies in learning to read, it seems that children make progress more quickly when the teacher actively involves them in determining their immediate learning goals (Schunk, 1987). Presumably the children then feel more committed to the goals and believe they are achieveable. We are all more inclined to respond positively to our own challenges rather than to satisfy requirements imposed upon us. So rather than just tell children every time what they must now do to make further progress, the teacher should try to find opportunities to discuss with them what the next step should be. The 'success book' idea outlined below in the next section would facilitate such discussion.

Having knowledge of your successes

It is not enough to have the opportunity to succeed, however. We must also know what constitutes success and the respects in which we have been successful. People sometimes say, 'She doesn't do justice to herself', or 'He's better than he realises', suggesting that it is possible to be successful and not really know it, or to dwell unduly on your failures and overlook what you have done well. Young children in particular need help in identifying the kinds of things in which success should be valued, in appreciating their assets, and in monitoring their own achievements. In this way they build up a clearer self-picture and can set themselves realistic challenges.

Gurney (1990) gives a number of strategies by which children can be encouraged to reflect upon their successes and assets. One is to get each child to keep a 'diary of good things'. As a way of helping pupils to appreciate their strengths and to counter self-denegratory tendencies, children can also make lists of the things they are good at and revise it at intervals. As Gurney points out, by keeping records of this kind, less confident children are able to remind themselves what they are good at, and teachers are provided with a useful source of material for individual or group discussion.

For these activities, it is important to encourage children to think in terms of their personal life and events outside the classroom, as well as formal school activities. These include not only clubs, hobbies, skills and talents but also personal deeds. Helping to care for a sick relative, befriending a lonely child or cheering up your mum are important human achievements which deserve recognition.

A more structured means of helping children to recognise their strengths and to share their efforts with others is the 'success book', as described by Coulby and Coulby (1990). A time is set aside each week for children to monitor and evaluate their achievements on prepared sheets which list selected aspects of school work and social activities plus one or two items which are special for each child (see figure 6.1). Once a week, the children rate their endeavours by drawing a star, smiley face or thumbs-down sign by each item. The teacher also tries to find time to talk to individuals about their evaluations so that general comments by the child and teacher can be added (see right-hand side of figure 6.1). Each child then takes the success book home for parents to add their comments, thus helping to set up important triangular relationships between pupil, teacher and parent. Although time-consuming, this device gives children a framework in which to identify their successes and efforts and to indicate areas in which more encouragement and support are needed.

Another interesting strategy is based on the theory that we can appreciate our own successes through what we say to ourselves about our own achievements. Citing successful experimental work, including his own with special needs pupils, Gurney (1990) argues that teachers should encourage individuals with low self-esteem to make positive self-referrent statements. He shows that teachers can train children to make positive comments about what they have achieved by praising or rewarding them for acknowledging their own efforts, for example by saying to the teacher 'I did well in maths today'.

Believing that others value you

All of us need to feel that our individuality is respected by those who are socially significant in our lives. Young children are especially

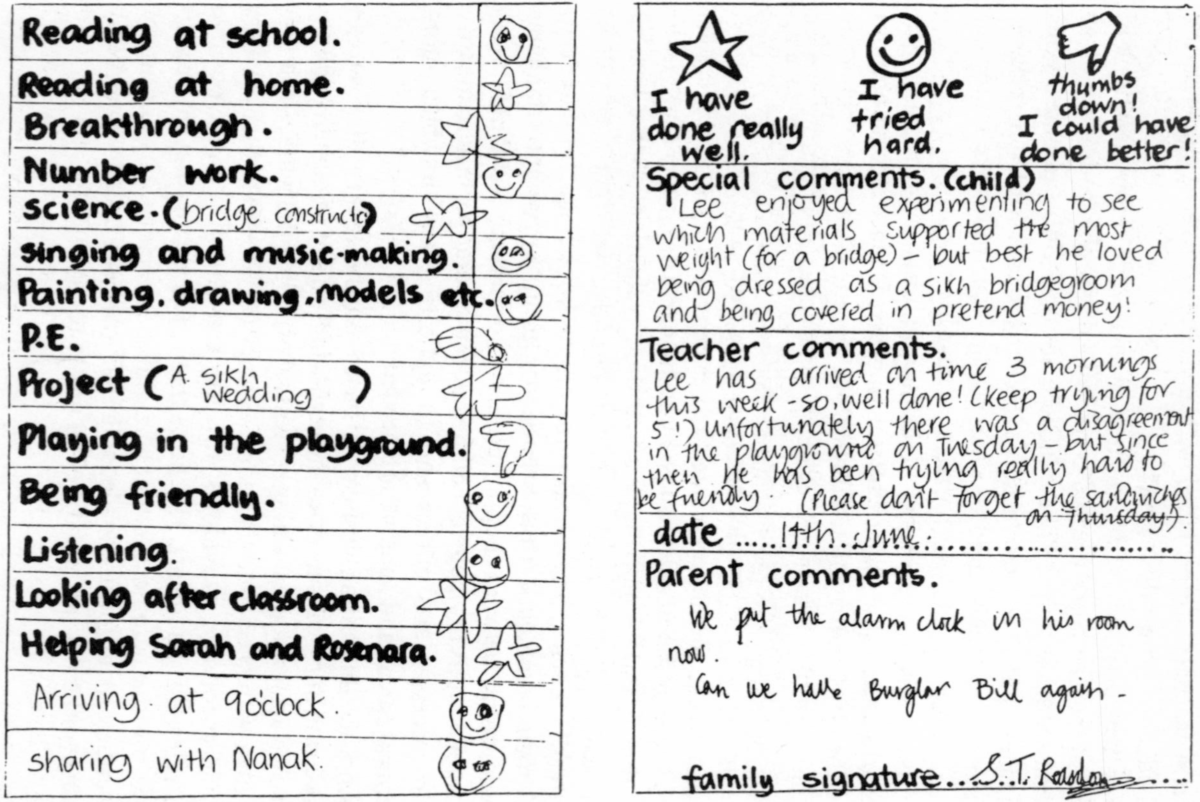

Reading at school.	
Reading at home.	
Breakthrough.	
Number work.	
Science. (bridge constructs)	
Singing and music-making.	
Painting, drawing, models etc.	
P.E.	
Project (A Sikh Wedding)	
Playing in the playground.	
Being friendly.	
Listening.	
Looking after classroom.	
Helping Sarah and Rosanara.	
Arriving at 9 o'clock.	
Sharing with Nanak.	

☆ I have done really well.

☺ I have tried hard.

👎 thumbs down! I could have done better!

Special comments. (child)
Lee enjoyed experimenting to see which materials supported the most weight (for a bridge) – but best he loved being dressed as a sikh bridegroom and being covered in pretend money!

Teacher comments.
Lee has arrived on time 3 mornings this week - so, well done! Keep trying for 5! Unfortunately there was a disagreement in the playground on Tuesday - but since then he has been trying really hard to be friendly. (Please don't forget the swimming on Thursday).

date ......14th June......

Parent comments.
We put the alarm clock in his room now.
Can we have Burglar Bill again -

family signature ...S.T.Rawler......

Figure 6.1 A page from a 'sourcebook'

dependent upon their relationships with adults and need to feel that the teacher is taking a personal interest in them, valuing their uniqueness and not seeing them as just a member of the group. Put another way, each child needs to feel that he or she matters. Apart from special activities of the kind described above, good teachers seize opportunities to get to know children through friendly chats both inside and outside the classroom. For instance, they ask about each child's likes and dislikes, hobbies and pastimes, skills and interests, family and pets. Here is an example of the way one teacher of a junior class does this in an almost incidental manner:

> As the children come into the room at the start of a session, I like to greet some by name – different children each time – and I try to follow up something they have previously mentioned to me. This morning, for instance, I was able to ask one child about her new baby brother and I asked another how she got on in her athletic club yesterday. This afternoon I asked a boy how he was feeling after an accident in the playground that morning. If somebody has done something special, I might tell the class so that their effort gets public recognition. But sometimes it's a quiet word that is needed. For example, there's one girl who's not happy with her step-mum and gets upset when she hasn't had a telephone call from her real mum who has left home. I also make a point of passing on the favourable remarks which other teachers make about individuals or the class.

Children also need a framework in which they are encouraged to acknowledge each other's attributes or good deeds. To help in this process, Leech and Wooster (1986) describe a game for young children which can be played for five or ten minutes at any convenient time during the day. The teacher will have prepared a box or bag of small cards containing the names of each child in the class. To start the game, the teacher draws two cards at random and reads out the names. The first named child is then asked to make a positive statement about the second. This procedure is repeated a few more times.

Having a strong sense of identity

Teachers can help to enhance children's sense of personal identity through activities which reinforce their self-awareness and sense of uniqueness. One approach is to get children to devise personal coats of arms, draw self-portraits or make advertisements about themselves. As Gurney (1990) comments, these activities can generate interesting display material and create opportunities for lively discussion about individual's personal attributes and achievements.

Enhancing feelings of confidence and competence

In this section, we consider the possibility that children's motivation to engage in curriculum activities and to feel competent is, in part, a consequence of the way they tend to explain their successes and failures. The kind of explanations which children give for doing well or badly affects their feelings of satisfaction and their degree of confidence about succeeding in the future. These considerations are related to a corpus of knowledge known as attribution theory.

Children often attribute their successes and failures to what they assume are their inherent abilities, for example when they make remarks such as 'I can't do sums' or 'I'm good at sport' or 'She is better than me at practical things'. As Schunk (1987) points out, beliefs in one's competence can affect behaviour. Pupils who hold doubts about their capability to learn will make little effort and try to avoid tasks which involve new learning, whereas those who have stronger beliefs about their competencies will be more motivated and therefore willing to put in more effort.

Weiner's attribution model

The work of Bernard Weiner and his colleagues has been particularly influential in relating attribution theory to educational contexts. Weiner (1979) explains how the explanations we give for our successes and failures can be classified in a number of ways. Three of these are particularly important:

(1) LOCUS OF CAUSALITY
This refers to whether we are attributing the event to something about ourselves (an *internal* attribution), such as ability, effort, mood, personality and state of health; or to something which lies outside ourselves (an *external* attribution), such as the difficulty of the task, how much help we were given, the conditions in which we are working, or just luck.

(2) STABILITY OVER TIME
This refers to the extent to which the factor is enduring, on the one hand, or subject to change on the other. For example, ability is regarded by most people as a fairly permanent characteristic; in contrast, our luck, or state of health, or the amount of effort we expend can go up and down.

(3) CONTROLLABILITY

This refers to the extent to which the factor can be controlled by our own violition. We can decide to try harder, for instance, or not to bother. But it is typically assumed that our general intelligence is not something that we can easily change by ourselves.

Now, it is part of Weiner's theory that the particular cause which an individual identifies as responsible for a successful or unsuccessful event has consequences for the prospect that individual holds about future performance. Consider, for example, two children, one of whom is successful and the other unsuccessful in a mathematics activity. Both, however attribute their experience to beliefs about their general ability or, more specifically, to ability in mathematics. The successful one says 'I'm good at all school subjects' or 'Anything to do with numbers comes easily to me', while the other says 'I think I must be stupid' or 'I'm no good at sums'. According to Weiner, the first child will feel confident about succeeding in future maths activities because ability is generally regarded as something fairly permanent and does not fluctuate from one moment to the next. For the same reason, however, the child who has not been successful will feel resigned to failing in the future: if ability is a 'fixed' quantity, what chance is there of ever doing well? Here lie the seeds of alienation and possibly disruptive behaviour.

But suppose that, instead of referring to their ability, each of the two children explain their experiences in terms of the amount of effort they have made. The successful child says 'It's because I tried really hard' and the unsuccessful one says 'Well, I didn't really try hard enough'. Then, argues Weiner, *both* children have reason to be optimistic about doing well next time because effort is both subject to change over time and can also (to a large extent) be controlled by the will. The child who was successful can reasonably assume that, by continuing to try hard, all will be well in the future. The child who failed can also believe that success is possible by making a bigger effort.

Children's changing understanding about ability and effort

Weiner's attribution model would seem to suggest that teachers should encourage children to attribute their successes either to trying hard or to having the requisite ability, and to attribute their failures to insufficient effort, not to lack of ability. Both ability and effort are internal attributions, but effort, unlike ability, can fluctuate and is controllable. For children who have not succeeded on a task, an attribution to effort therefore has motivational potential, whereas an attribution to ability would lead to lack of confidence.

Although, as we shall see, this may be a helpful approach to the problem of pupil motivation, applying this model to primary school pupils is not a straightforward matter because Weiner's studies were with older pupils and adults. Recent attributional studies involving younger children have produced two particularly interesting sorts of findings in this respect.

The first is that pre-adolescent children use a more extensive range of attributions than Weiner allowed for. A British study by Little (1985) has shown that children between the ages of 5 and 14 years certainly refer a great deal to ability and effort when explaining success and failure, but they refer also to other factors such as whether they muck around, whether they work too fast or too slowly, and how much time they spend on an activity. Also, unlike adults, they apparently make little reference to the difficulty of the task or to luck.

Secondly, there are developmental changes in children's attributional styles. In Little's study, the 5-year-olds would often explain a success simply by describing it. For example, when invited to explain why one child had painted a better picture than another, a girl said 'The nice one is much nicer and the horrible one, it's much horribler'! However, as children move up the primary school they make more attributions to specific and general competence. Thus they talk about 'knowing how to do sums' or 'being clever'. Most of all they come to realise the importance of effort and taking an interest in their work: the 5-year-olds seldom used effort in their explanations.

Findings about children's developing understanding of the role of ability and effort has also been noted in some American studies. Nicholls (1983), for example, found that children in the very early years of schooling assume that success, ability and effort go together. For them, people who work hard are people who are good at things and are successful, and those who do not make an effort are stupid and unsuccessful. Trying hard is thus a sign of being clever. During their early junior years, pupils come to realise that even stupid people can sometimes be successful and clever people can fail. Ability is now seen as something separate from effort, though still not as a 'fixed' characteristic. Pupils at this age assume that by working harder they will actually get more clever! It is not until the last year of primary or early years of secondary school that children come to adopt the prevalent adult view that no amount of effort can improve one's ability, which sets limits to what one is capable of doing.

So what should teachers do?

Following Nicholls' findings, it might be tempting for the teacher of young primary children to think that it makes no difference whether she encourages her pupils to attribute their failures to lack of ability or to lack of effort, for children around 7 or 8 years seem to think that one's ability can be improved by trying harder. However, Colin Rogers (1990) has argued that this conclusion would be unwarranted. For if children get into the *habit* of explaining personal failure in terms of a low level of ability, this will have adverse effects on their beliefs about the prospects of future success when, in later years, they come to regard ability as a stable factor. It is thus very important for teachers to be sensitive to children's attribution styles, even during the infant and early junior years of schooling, because these have important implications for educational success later on, if not at the time.

The important issue for teachers, then, concerns the extent to which they can encourage children to hold beliefs about their personal competence which will help them to remain optimistic about future success. From reviews of literature in this area (Bar-Tal, 1982; Rogers, 1987 and 1990; Schunk, 1987), it seems that, while competence beliefs and attribution style are partly dispositional and cultural matters, they are also subject to the individual's experiences of success and failure. Evidence cited by these authors points clearly to the fact that teachers can and do influence pupils' attributions, feelings of confidence, and beliefs in their general and specific competencies. Four influencing factors seem particularly important:

(1) OPPORTUNITIES FOR FREQUENT SUCCESS

Children are more likely to judge themselves efficacious if they experience success more often than failure. The more a child experiences success, the more that child will assume this is due to his or her own ability and not just to hard work (Rogers, 1990; Schunk, 1987). Conversely, the less failure is the rule, the more inclined will the child be to put lack of success down to lack of effort. Hence once again, we see the importance of the teacher creating regular opportunities for success. This includes matching work to children's previous achievements, communicating positive expectations, presenting complicated material in short and manageable chunks, and providing chances for children to experience success in a variety of activities (see discussion above, pp. 79–81).

(2) FEEDBACK ABOUT CHILDREN'S WORK

What teachers say to pupils about their work seems likely to influence attributions. From our previous discussion, it would appear that teachers should attribute successes to the child's ability ('Good, Angela, you can do it!') and failures to lack of effort ('I know you can do it, Andrew, if you try'), for this should help children to be confident about future progress. Schunk (1987) argues that, once the pupil who has experienced failure begins to show improvement, the teacher should communicate her belief in the child's ability rather than effort. This would suggest shifting from remarks like 'That's good. You're really working hard' to 'You're good at this, aren't you?'. This is because a pupil who is succeeding and regularly told that success depends on trying hard may wonder why so much effort is required to get anywhere, and see this as a sign of low natural ability.

Another point here concerns the things that teachers criticise children for. Some children attract little general criticism from their teachers because they are well-behaved and tidy, but they get criticised specifically for poor work. According to Carol Dweck (1985), girls are particularly vulnerable to this kind of treatment in the early years of schooling. Apparently, when children are praised for matters of form, such as neatness, but in contrast are subjected to criticism about the content of their work, they may well assume that they lack the necessary ability to succeed in the curriculum area under question. This is particularly so in subjects such as mathematics where it is generally assumed that success depends on general ability (Rogers, 1990). This may not lead to disruptive behaviour, but it could well result in feelings of helplessness.

(3) THE RISKS OF TOO MUCH COMPETITION

Classroom climate also makes a big difference. An element of competition can be helpful for children's motivation, provided that the same people do not always win. The chances of success must therefore be realistic for all the competitors. Rogers (1990) comments that an unduly competitive atmosphere, such as that created by regular whole-class tests, encourages the idea that both success and failure depend on a high degree of general ability. It also discourages the development of intrinsic interest in classroom activities and instead encourages a fear of failure and a dependence on external rewards or sanctions.

(4) CHOICE OF PUPILS TO DEMONSTRATE SKILLS

Teachers often make use of pupils to demonstrate skills and help those experiencing difficulty. In terms of improving pupils' beliefs about their abilities, this has some justification. The question is whether it is a good idea for teachers to choose the most skilful pupils to demonstrate. This may not be the best strategy since those who are unsure of themselves may feel unable to emulate the skills of a typically confident performer (Schunk, 1987).

Suppose during a swimming lesson a teacher wants a child to demonstrate how to dive into the pool. It would be tempting to ask the best diver, but it might be better to use a pupil who had only recently acquired the confidence and skill to dive successfully. The same idea could be applied to other curriculum areas. The best child to demonstrate, say, subtraction might be one who had recently been experiencing difficulty but had now got the hang of it. The point is that children are likely to feel more confident about their own capabilities if they see themselves as personally similar to the child demonstrating.

Taking the trouble to enable pupils to feel worthy, confident and competent should reduce feelings of 'learned helplessness' or the need to 'act out' in order to compensate for a perceived inability to cope with school work. In the next chapter, this idea is applied more directly to problems of inter-pupil behaviour by indicating ways in which teachers can help children to develop greater confidence in managing their personal relationships and feel less need to resort to aggression.

Chapter 7

Managing Pupils' Behaviour Towards each other

> In the course of their duties around the school, the vast majority . . . of primary teachers reported pupils showing a lack of concern for others.
>
> *Elton Report, p. 241*

The management of pupil behaviour is not only about teacher-pupil relationships, but also about relationships between pupils. Although the Elton Inquiry research found that aggression towards teachers was rare, aggression by primary school pupils towards each other was common. Eight out of ten teachers reported that they had seen at least one incident of unruly or aggressive behaviour in the corridor or playground during the previous week; and physical aggression between pupils was nominated by primary teachers as the most, or next most, difficult problem with which they had to deal outside the classroom.

To some extent, the way pupils treat each other in the school depends on how they are treated by the teachers. This is one reason why it is important for teachers to set a good model in the way they try to resolve conflict in the classroom, demonstrating how it is possible to be assertive without being aggressive. Hence the importance of voice control, body language, and the manner of reprimanding and punishing.

However, more direct strategies are also needed to heighten children's awareness of their emotions and reactive behaviour in confrontations, and to help them develop the skills involved in behaving cooperatively. In this chapter we consider some of the ways in which teachers can help to improve children's inter-personal behaviour.

Promoting understanding of behaviour

It is sometimes assumed that helping children to relate better to each other is mainly an 'extra-curricular' activity, something that is pursued outside the mainstream curriculum or in school clubs and on school journeys. Certainly extra-curricular activities provide excellent opportunities for social learning and the development of cooperative attitudes, but it is important also to regard these aspects of children's education as an intrinsic part of regular classroom work.

Most primary school teachers believe that a key role in their job as educators is to develop children's understanding. As is often said, the emphasis is as much on the process of learning as on the product. Yet in the case of their inter-personal behaviour, the promotion of children's understanding is frequently overlooked. Timothy Daux, an American teacher working in London, believes that children can gradually learn to become less aggressive towards each other if they are encouraged to reflect upon their emotions and reactions to situations in which they would ordinarily hit out physically or verbally. He has therefore developed strategies which promote young children's understanding of inappropriate behaviour and which give opportunities to demonstrate this understanding in practice. As children begin to comprehend, he argues, they slowly learn to assume responsibility for their actions.

Among the techniques which Daux (1988) has identified are the following:

(1) TEACHING CHILDREN POSITIVE STRATEGIES FOR DEALING WITH CONFRONTIVE SITUATIONS

Through weekly class discussion and role play, Daux helps children to understand that we all have a need to gain attention from others and to assert ourselves, but that some people are better than others in satisfying this need without resorting to physical violence and verbal conflict. What Daux does is to present everyday situations to the class and ask 'What could you do?', thus encouraging children to explore alternative ways of seeking attention and responding to 'negative attention'. Examples are how to borrow something from another child, how to share limited resources such as a playground skipping rope, and how to respond to teasing or hitting. Not surprisingly, the children do not change their response patterns immediately, but they gradually learn to do so as they build up a repertoire of courses of action and are encouraged by their teacher to try these out as opportunities arise.

(2) CREATING OPPORTUNITIES FOR POWER SHARING

A rota is used to give each child in the class the opportunity to assume a leadership function. These include dismissing the class, collecting and recording money for trips, leading a class discussion, directing clean-up chores, guiding visitors round the school. Children are also encouraged to place ideas in a suggestion box for the better functioning of the class, and these are then discussed. This encourages the class to address problems in a positive fashion rather than by blaming and criticising.

(3) EMPOWERING THE VICTIM OF AGGRESSION

When children pick on each other, the teacher draws the attention of the whole class to the situation and later makes a point of enquiring in class about the victim's well-being:

> When teachers model concern for the victim of teasing and aggression, observant children develop the same supportive actions. Additionally and importantly, the aggressor is denied the attention or power which might have been gained at the expense of the victim. (p. 71)

Playground behaviour

Many teachers are worried about what they see as the declining quality of behaviour in the playground. In one of the few studies in this area, Peter Blatchford (1989) interviewed primary school staff in thirteen LEAs throughout the south-east of England, identifying problems and pointing to possible solutions. He found that teachers complained not only about physical aggression and fighting but about name-calling, verbal abuse, racist and sexist remarks, petty squabbling, the strain on lunchtime supervisors and the decline in traditional games and rhymes. Girls and the younger children seemed to be particularly vulnerable, with boys and older children dominating playground space with football. There was a special problem of bullying, an issue which we discuss in the next section.

Among the strategies which schools had initiated to deal with playground behaviour problems, Blatchford found the following:

(1) A CLEAR SET OF RULES AND SANCTIONS

These define what is acceptable and unacceptable in the playground and help to get across the seriousness of inconsiderate and dangerous behaviour. The rules of one school focussed on certain specific matters – for example there was to be no punching, hitting, climbing on other children's backs or swearing – and ended with a rule which tried to reduce thoughtless, impulsive behaviour: 'Ask yourself whether you would like it done or said to you. If not, don't do it'. At this school, the teachers agreed a common policy for responding to infringements. For instance, for a first offence the child would be reminded of the rules and their name noted: a serious offence after several infringements might involve contact with the parents or losing playtime.

(2) CAREFUL MONITORING OF PLAYGROUND BEHAVIOUR

For instance, in one school, the head found that behaviour improved through keeping a record of incidents and the action taken, and reporting these to parents in a newsletter and to the children in assembly. In another school, the aggressors were asked to act as the playground monitors, with responsibility for protecting the victims.

(3) ENCOURAGING POSITIVE BEHAVIOUR IN THE PLAYGROUND

This included playground supervisors praising loudly incidents of good behaviour whilst quietly reprimanding offenders, and discussing examples, of pro-social play in school assembly.

(4) DISSCUSSING THE PROBLEM OF FOOTBALL WITH CHILDREN

The objective was to enable boys, who tend to dominate the space, to see the problem from the girls' point of view. Schools did not find it easy to resolve the problem of equal opportunities in this context, but found it useful to try out different plans and discuss their effectiveness with the children. For example, after much experimentation, one school found that limiting the use of large balls to the morning playtime was the most acceptable solution.

(5) WHOLE-SCHOOL POLICIES WHICH TAKE A CLEAR MORAL STAND AGAINST RACIST AND SEXIST BEHAVIOUR

The staff in some schools issued regular reminders to make clear to all pupils that name-calling, violence and verbal abuse would not be tolerated. At the same time, it was appreciated that manifestations of racism and sexism in the playground should not be tackled in isolation from their occurrence elsewhere, and that whole-school policies need to ensure that these issues permeate the school curriculum.

(6) ALTERING PLAYGROUND ARRANGEMENTS

Staggering playtimes helped to reduce the numbers in the playground at any one time and increase supervision ratios. Making separate provision for the youngest children was one way in which some schools gave these children special protection. One school paired classes of younger and older children, and found that the younger ones benefited from the protection provided, and the older ones from exercising this responsibility. Other schools found that bullying could be reduced at the start of the day by allowing early arrivals to enter the school right away and engage in quiet activities.

These are just some of the main strategies which Blatchford found. Others included improving the quality of play through improved playground resources and encouraging cooperative games, developing a cross-curricular project on playtime, and involving lunchtime supervisors in decision-making about playground policy and the offer of training in child management. The book is full of interesting ideas, and is recommended reading.

Pat White (1988), an education lecturer, has described a playground project which she helped to organise in Laycock Primary School in an educational priority area of London. This not only involved all teaching and support staff but also generated a high level of pupil involvement, with some participation from parents too. Children discussed their playground experiences and feelings with their teachers, and then wrote and drew about them. The material revealed many sad instances of 'preventable misery and distress, ... petty spitefulness and unpleasantness' (p. 195) which suggested that any effort to ameliorate such suffering would be worthwhile. Additionally, two representatives from each class compiled summmaries of the children's perceptions. At a parents' evening, some children acted out mini-dramas of playground conflict, and the parents discussed the issues raised.

A playground code was then drawn up and went through several drafts during the course of discussions with the staff. The final version (pp. 197–8) read:

1. We will always be kind and considerate to everybody in the playground.
2. We will look after the playground and make sure that it is always a nice place to be in.
3. We will share the playground space so that other games, besides football, can be played.
4. Even if we are in the midst of something very exciting or important, we will stop and listen to any instructions an adult may give us.

At an earlier stage in the project, football had been limited to certain times during the week, but it was later decided to give children (with whom the matter had been discussed) the opportunity to share space themselves. The code was reinforced through praising good behaviour during play periods, entering the names of offenders in a book, and inviting the parents of children with repeated entries to talk about the problem. White was concerned to provide opportunities in which children could reflect about their experiences, so the teachers organised 'awareness sessions' in which children discussed problematic playground situations and what their response should be.

Involving staff and pupils in exercises of this kind makes astonishingly heavy demands on staff time, with a succession of meetings after school. But the process of general participation itself seems to contribute to resolving the problems. Two other case studies in pupil involvement which include playground behaviour are given below (pp. 100–103 and 115–121).

Bullying

By bullying is meant not only physical aggression between a dominant pupil and a sufferer, but also malicious teasing, name-calling and harassment, ostracising individuals from the group, intimidation and attempts at extortion. Tattum and Herbert (1990) define bullying simply as 'the wilful, conscious desire to hurt, threaten or frighten someone'.

Compared with behaviour problems which directly confront teachers and parents, the subject of bullying has received little attention. The Elton Report devotes only three paragraphs to it. British studies published during the 1980s, however, have shown that physical and psychological violence between children is on a larger scale at each age level than was previously assumed. In a sample of 700 11-year-olds, the Newsons (1984) found that over a quarter of mothers said that their children were bullied at school and over a fifth said they were bullied in the street. A larger and more recent survey among 1078 Cleveland pupils in their final year of primary school revealed that almost a quarter of children were either bullies or victims or both (Stephenson and Smith, 1987). The researchers also found that the problem usually persisted over some years, suggesting that bullying was not just a phase which would disappear spontaneously. On the other hand, it was much less of an issue in some primary schools than others, the least trouble occuring when the staff had developed clearly understood policies.

During the mid-1980s, Michele Elliott, in a project for Kidscape (an organisation set up to protect children from abuse), invited 4000 children between 5 and 16 to express their worries and concerns. The majority talked about bullying, most referring to incidents instigated by an older child and taking place in unsupervised parts of school, while travelling to and from school, or in other places where no adult was around. Some victims were so terrified that they would stay off school. Two-thirds of the victims and eight of out ten bullies were boys.

The first British book on bullying was published in 1988 by Tattum and Lane, and others quickly followed (Roland and Munthe 1989; Besag, 1989). Between them, these give an exhaustive review of the problem, drawing on evidence and experience from abroad as well as in the U. K. Suggestions for schools can be found in these volumes and elsewhere; (particulars in Further Reading at the end of this book). Here we draw attention to some of the principal ideas which illustrate the need for teachers, parents and pupils to work closely together.

The problems of bullying must be tackled on three fronts: general preventive measures, protection of the victims, and strategies for dealing with the bullies themselves.

Preventive strategies

It will be recalled that, from evidence revealed in the Cleveland Study, bullying is less evident in schools which have not dismissed the problem as a phase of growing up, but have developed well-articulated policies. Amongst these is an unequivocal statement in the school rules, backed up by regular reminders to pupils and parents, that bullying will not be tolerated and that offenders will be dealt with firmly. Besag (1989) suggests that all but the most determined bullies are likely to be deterred if it is known that parents and school governors will be informed of any incidents.

Teachers are often unaware about the extent of bullying, partly because the victims are often too frightened or embarrassed to say anything and partly because many incidents occur outside the school grounds and when pupils are walking to and from school. In school, it is obviously important to be vigilant in the playground and around the buildings, but attention also needs to be given to the ethos of classrooms and the school in general. This points to the importance of strategies, such as those discussed in Chapter 6, which help children to feel that they belong to a caring community and are not subjected to feelings of isolation or are under unfair pressure due to competition. Teachers can also help to raise levels of awareness and create a common concern about bullying by conducting surveys of pupil aggression with their class. The results are then discussed during lesson time and at assembly, while teachers discuss findings with parents at class meetings (Tattum, 1989).

To reduce bullying both inside and outside school, liaison with parents is essential to ensure that the responsibility is a joint one and that the children receive the same messages. However, care must be taken to dissuade parents from adopting bullying tactics themselves since, as we saw in Chapter 5, severe or unreasonable punishment can exacerbate behaviour problems. Roland (1989) urges class teachers to arrange meetings, outings and other occasions which help parents to get to know each other well. A close network helps parents to adopt more effective child-rearing strategies and to pass on to children common expectations for behaviour. Parents can also boost non-aggressive behaviour by arranging for their children to experience rewarding relationships in tutoring or caring for younger members of the family (Stephenson and Smith, 1989).

Protecting and supporting victims

The first requirement in giving support to victims is to get across the message that the staff are 'listening' teachers and that they wish to bring the subject of bullying out into the open. Adults sometimes give children the impression that it is not 'done' to express strong feelings, especially about one's personal fears and worries. Even more commonly, children are discouraged from informing adults about bullying on the gounds that 'telling' on others is wrong. All too often, however, these messages are recipes for misery. Victims must know that teachers will take them seriously. Additionally, as the Elton Committee recommended, all children must be encouraged to tell staff about incidents which they have witnessed or have reason to suspect. Teachers also need to be sensitive to signs of possible bullying, such as children becoming more withdrawn or staying away from school.

The subject of bullying needs to be given a high profile in the classroom. Through role-play, discussion, literature and writing, children should be given opportunities to express their feelings about bullying and make suggestions for action. Such strategies can sometimes enable those who bully to feel the weight of peer pressure as well as giving reassurance to victims that the class is on their side.

Teachers sometimes dismiss reports of bullying by believing that the victim 'brought it on' by behaving provocatively. Indeed, the 'just world' theory (Lerner, 1970) holds that there is a self-defensive tendency in most of us to tolerate suffering by believing that the sufferers are at fault and deserve their misfortune. The evidence suggests, however, that the great majority of bullied children are weak and ineffectual individuals, though a minority are confident and seek out aggressive situations (Stephenson and Smith, 1989). This means that victims can often be helped through strategies which make them less of an easy prey – boosting the weaker children's confidence, self-esteem, and assertiveness and helping isolated children to make friends.

Dealing with children who bully

Since the personality of the bully is a complex phenomenon, the way to deal with offenders is not a straightforward matter. The general principle is to take action which makes an unequivocal stand, but is also constructive and does not drive the child to 'take it out' on the victim. Sufferers often bear their agony in secret because of this fear.

The first step is to find out the facts of the matter. This can be difficult since often there are no witnesses to incidents, and distressed children sometimes pretend they have been bullied as a way of 'getting at' those they dislike. One tactic is to ask responsible pupils to shadow victims.

Once children who have been bullying are identified, the action taken must be firm but positive. Although a minority of bullies are anxious individuals, the majority are confident and tough, possessing strong impulses to dominate others and finding it difficult to control their aggressive tendencies (Olweus, 1978). Children who bully therefore need to feel pressure from peers as well as adults to inhibit their bullying tendencies.

One technique is for the school to set up a court in which the children are the judges. Kidscape recommends this approach and suggests that the court comprises two pupils elected by their peers and two by the staff, with one teacher also attending. At its weekly meetings, the court would decide on solutions and penalties within a framework previously agreed by the whole school. There is evidence to suggest that this can be an effective measure (Laslett, 1982), and some individual teachers have used it at class level (see case study that follows). Children who bully are less able to thrive on their 'macho' image if they feel that their actions are condemned not only by the staff, but by the school as a whole.

At the same time it is important to ensure that offenders are not simply deterred, but helped to become more integrated into the school community. Everyone must try to spell out that it is the bullying *behaviour* that is unacceptable, not the child as a person. Teachers can act positively by encouraging the offender to see things from the victim's standpoint and to cooperate in supporting the victim. The line to take is 'I think you can help us do something to help X. What do you suggest? Let's see what we can work out together'.

The involvement of parents is also important. Tattum and Herbert (1990) suggest that teachers should keep records of their discussions with the bully and the victim, send a report to the bully's parent and ask for a response in writing. The report should then be kept with the pupils' files for a specified time. Although many parents are anxious to help and look to the school for support, the root of the trouble is sometimes parents who themselves are abusive and offer a model of aggression (Besag, 1989). The teacher therefore needs to discuss positive strategies with the parents, such as praising the child at each sign of pro-social behaviour towards the victim and regulating the child's 'natural' rewards (e.g. pocket money, watching TV, playing with friends) accordingly. Young children who bully do not always appreciate the effect of their actions, or the unfairness and unkindness of making fun of children with ailments or handicaps or who are of a different race or culture. Teachers can encourage parents to talk about these matters, encouraging the child to empathise with the victim.

A case study in playground behaviour and bullying

Although ideally the problems of playground behaviour and bullying should be addressed in whole-school policies (see next chapter) the absence of a collaborative approach does not prevent the class teacher making some headway. As an illustration, we give here an account of the work undertaken by one infant teacher who undertook an anti-bullying project with her class of 5-to 6-year-olds, and who wrote a report about her work as part of the requirements for an in-service BEd degree (Belilios, 1990).

Although the school in question was a small private institution for boys aged 4 to 9 who came from middle-class homes, the parents and pupils had expressed concern about the frequency of aggressive behaviour and harassment (by gangs as well as individuals) and a succession of 'accidental' playground injuries. The staff were also concerned that playground incidents were affecting classroom work and that some children were gaining reputations for being bullies or victims.

The teacher began by making a record of observations whilst on playground duty. She noticed, for instance, how football and chasing games monopolised playground space and were the cause of frequent accidents. There was also much role-play in which the boys acted out aggressive TV heroes, but virtually no structured or traditional games. She then decided to involve the class in discussion about group behaviour in the playground. A number of problems soon emerged. One was the lack of communication between groups. One boy said: 'We have two teams. We're the goodies, we chase them and trap them and take them to our dungeons. But they don't know what we're playing.' Another problem was that groups would sometimes insist on a particular individual joining in against his will, or prevent him playing as he wanted to. The children also gave several examples of deliberate, unkind acts. One complained: 'I don't like kicking – lots of people do it – I don't know why'.

The teacher followed up this discussion by asking the boys to write down rules which would help to make the playground a happier place. These were subsequently discussed and formed the basis of an agreed code of conduct which was displayed on the classroom wall together with the children's individual suggestions. The code was given the title 'Let's have fun in the playground', and the rules decided upon were as follows:

– We'll be kind in what we do and say

- We'll tell others what we're playing
- We won't make others do things they don't want to
- We'll try to play team games not gang games
- If we're a leader, we'll try to guide our team carefully and remember to think of other people's feelings.

Further observations in the playground suggested that the exercise had helped to improve the quality of play among members of this class.

In addition to her general playground observations, the teacher made detailed recordings about the behaviour of three boys in her class (here referred to as Gary, Bob and Mark) whom she considered to be 'at risk' in different respects.

Gary, although only 5, showed signs of developing into a physical bully. In the playground he would compensate for his difficulty in achieving social integration by pushing his way into groups. Moreover, he seemed unaware of the social unacceptability of his behaviour, in spite of the negative reaction of the other children who frequently complained about his actions. He was the only boy who did not personally relate to the classroom discussion, appearing to be unaware that many general remarks were in fact directed at him.

When Gary was later caught hitting another boy on the head with a stick, he appeared to have no conscience about the hurt inflicted, although he admitted the offence. At this point the teacher decided to try using a children's court, following her reading of a successful experiment conducted by Laslett (1982) in a school for maladjusted children. The class elected three of their number to be judges, choosing individuals who had a reputation for being fair and thoughtful. The victim presented his evidence, and Gary made little attempt to defend his action.

The judges then retired outside the room and came to four decisions. One was to inform Gary's parents. Interestingly, the children wanted to do this themselves, though in the event the teacher decided it would be better if she undertook this responsibility. The children also decided that Gary should lose three playtimes (the loss of one on a previous occasion clearly not being sufficient), to keep him under surveillance and to inform the teacher of any further bullying.

The decision to allow such young children to hold their own court had not been taken lightly. Even though the teacher was present throughout, she was worried about possible deterimental effects of Gary's self-esteem. However she was persuaded by Laslett's argument that the experience gives children practice in shared responsibility, and that there was clearly a need to take action which dramatically impressed upon Gary the influence which his behaviour was having on other children. In the event, the teacher's fears were allayed. The class took their responsibilties very seriously, and their decision did prove to be effective in reducing the problem. The teacher writes:

> Gary was chastened by the peer ruling . . . He became more aware of his actions in the playground. The class accepted more responsibility for his behaviour and encouraged him generally. Their interest led to his greater involvement in group activities and he generally became more socially integrated with the others. Comments like, 'Hey Gary that's really good' and 'Let's have a look, Gary' were encouraging and indicated the extent of his acceptance within the group. (p. 16)

Bob was a 6-year-old intelligent boy 'at risk' of developing into a verbal bully. He would use his powers of articulation to tease and taunt others by calling them names, picking in particular on one boy, Mark (see below), whom he called 'poo face' and 'smelly pants'. Mark would help to maintain this behaviour by invariably 'rising' to it with helpless response such as 'I'm not! I'm not, am I?'

The teacher decided to organise a class discussion about name-calling. Several children demonstrated their ability to empathise with victims, for example:

> 'When you call people names you upset them'
> 'I feel that people are bullying when they are calling other people names'
> 'People call people names and think they are clever but they are getting more spiteful'.

The class then decided that, although boys who called others names may not mean what they said, name-calling was hurtful and unkind. It was agreed that name-callers should be ignored, but that adults should be informed. Some boys suggested that a suitable punishment would be to stop culprits from watching TV 'so they don't copy rude words', but retracted this later on the grounds that 'some programmes help us learn'! The children eventually agreed that persistent name-callers should be reported to the head and that incidents should be talked about in class.

The outcome of the discussion was encouraging, heightening awareness of the effects of name-calling and severely curtailing its practice – though the teacher realised that she would need to hold further class discussions to sustain the new understanding.

Mark was a 5-year-old boy of small stature who was in danger of developing into a victim of bullying. His attempts to retaliate by announcing in a high-pitched voice 'Don't touch me or I'll scream' simply caused amusement and encouraged further provocation. The teacher noticed that Mark was a loner at playtime, and would frequently return to the classroom early to avoid the rejection of others. Pairing him with another isolated boy did not seem to help in this instance. By maintaining observations, however, the teacher hit upon a successful intervention strategy.

In the school library, Mark showed a preference for books on hospitals and sometimes came to school with a first aid kit which he used in the playground to offer assistance (rather bossily) with pupils who were hurt. The teacher used this knowledge to engage the class in discussion about caring attitudes, and made a point of drawing attention to Mark's helpfulness when a child had a nose-bleed and another suffered a playground injury. Further observation suggested that the class now seemed to adopt a more positive stance towards Mark and accepted his tendency to be bossy as a desire to help – although, again, the teacher realised that more work would need to be done to help Mark develop a positive identity.

As this study illustrates, a primary class teacher can play a major role in identifying children who are 'at risk' of becoming bullies or victims, and in developing positive strategies to intervene at an early stage. The key measures in this case appeared to be three-fold: (i) close observation in the playground to note individual and group problems, (ii) class discussion to raise the children's consciousness of the effects of their behaviour on others, and (iii) the provision of a framework in which the children cooperate in drawing up their own code of conduct, suggesting intervention measures, supporting vulnerable children, and exercising pressure on the culprits.

Managing cooperative learning

It is a mistake to think that the personal-social development of children and their academic education are necessarily separate activities which should be pursued on separate occasions. In many lessons the emphasis will be more on one than the other; but, as numerous research studies in the United States have shown, cooperative learning situations, in which children work collaboratively in pairs or small groups, appears to provide optimum conditions for promoting *both* academic *and* social objectives.

In a review of 122 studies which compared the effects of cooperative, competitive and individualistic classroom learning environments, Johnson and Johnson (1982) concluded that cooperative strategies at all levels not only promote higher academic achievement but also more constructive relationships between children:

> The use of cooperative learning strategies enables educators to 'have their cake and eat it too' by simultaneously promoting high achievement, constructive student-student relationships, positive attitudes towards subject areas, continuing motivation, critical thinking, high quality reasoning strategies, cooperative competencies and psychological health. (p. 12)

It is one thing for the teacher to accept the need for cooperative learning and to set up cooperative learning situations, but quite another to know how to encourage children to *be* cooperative. As we saw in Chapter 3 (p. 42), just seating children round tables will not guarantee constructive collaboration and may even facilitate bad behaviour. The teacher therefore has to *plan* for cooperative learning experiences.

There are few British studies which have explored the process by which children learn to cooperate in group work, but we shall consider two of these. The first concerns the make-up of groups for cooperative learning, and the second concerns the teacher's role in providing constructive feedback.

In one small-scale investigation, Bennett and Cass (1988) explored the effects of grouping children according to different ability criteria. Working in an urban middle school with groups of 11–12-year-olds, each made up of two boys and a girl or two girls and a boy, they compared the children's interactive processes and understanding when working with a computer program about Saxon settlement patterns. The task involved having to make a number of decisions inferred from general principles.

The researchers found that in all groups, no matter what the ability mix, the on-task behaviour was noticeably high. The children were clearly motivated by this mode of working. However, there were differences in the quality of interaction and levels of understanding. As might be expected, high attainers performed well in these respects, whether working together in a single ability group or as individuals in mixed ability groups. However, cooperative acivity in general was least satisfactory in groups of all-average or all-low attainers or in groups comprising a high, an average and a low attainer. In contrast, the interaction and understanding in groups made up of one high and two low attainers was impressive. One low and two high attainers was less satisfactory, the low attainer tending to be ignored or to opt out.

The logistics of the ordinary classroom obviously place constraints on ways in which groups can be made up, but, on this limited evidence, the teacher would be wise to take care over group composition and to experiment with different configurations. In particular, in the interests of furthering cooperation between children of different attainment levels, it would seem advisable to find opportunities for placing two low attainers with one high. In another study, two teachers and a lecturer (Burden et al., 1988) found that, with 6-year-olds, neither size of group nor sex compostition made any difference in the ability of children to cooperate. It may be, therefore, that the juxtaposition of children is more important with older primary groups.

The Burden et al. study also looked more closely at the role of the teacher in promoting cooperation in a range of collaborative activities such as problem-solving, discussion of a poem, and discussion about what to do in problematic moral situations. The management problem which the investigators explored concerned strategies for providing feedback which would help children to *become aware* of those features of their behaviour which were either helping or hindering cooperative activity. Such strategies included: being prepared to question; encouraging quiet members to speak; challenging others to think again; reminding the group of instructions; suggesting alternative approaches; explaining your thinking to others. Working with groups of four children aged 9 to 11 years, the teachers played back recordings of group talk or provided transcripts for the children to read. This certainly stimulated interest:

> When the children saw the transcription for the first time they were fascinated. Their initial reactions were surprise and disbelief, for example, 'Did I really say that?'. These reactions gave way to the beginnings of self-review, for example, 'Oh! goodness, I talk too much', 'Poor Mark's trying to say something again'.

Over a six-week period, the children were taught to recognise for themselves the skills needed for successful cooperative group work. In later stages, the teacher would stop the tape (sometimes in response to the children's initiative) in order to elicit suggestions about what was helping or hindering cooperative activity. Although this too was a small-scale study, the results demonstrated how, through feedback of tape-recordings of group discussion, teachers can promote group collaboration by developing children's self-awareness of their actions and sensitivity to others in the group.

Apart from using collaborative learning strategies in regular curriculum areas, teachers can engage children in special games which promote cooperative activity. There are on the market a number of books which describe these approaches, and suggestions are included under 'Further Reading' at the end of this book.

Chapter 8

Working Collaboratively with Colleagues, Parents and Pupils

↗ spiel

> The most effective schools seem to be those that have created a positive
> atmosphere based on a sense of community and shared values.
> *Elton Report, pp. 12–13*

In the last chapter, it was noted how problems of playground behaviour and bullying are best tackled by the staff acting as a team and eliciting the active cooperation of pupils and parents. As the Elton Report importantly noted, standards of school behaviour are most effectively improved when all members of the school community feel positively involved. The last chapter in this book therefore looks in more detail at some of the ways in which teachers can cooperate with each other, with parents and with pupils to bring about high standards of behaviour.

Peer support groups

The tradition whereby teachers bear their discipline problems in isolation is fortunately being eroded in many schools. As the Elton Committee noted, the problem revolves around the question of professional pride: 'Too often teachers do not seek help because it feels like an admission of incompetence, and they do not offer it because it feels like accusing a colleague of incompetence' (DES, 1989, p. 69). But coping alone is stressful, and if that stress is communicated to the children, it may help to maintain the problem behaviour.

Of course, teachers have always turned to senior colleagues for help, but not always constructively. One practice has been to send pupils who are disruptive to the head or deputy. However 'referral upwards' needs to operate within a clear code of practice if it is not to be abused.

Further, asking the head to take all responsibility does nothing to improve the class teacher's group management skills or position of authority. Teachers need the kind of support which helps to make them more effective managers of pupil behaviour. This is where peer support comes in.

The Elton team envisaged that in every school an informal and voluntary facility would be provided whereby teachers would offer each other mutual support by meeting regularly, on the basis of equality, to discuss their management practices. One member of the group would agree to act as a facilitator. A peer support group does not replace time spent at formal staff meetings talking about behaviour policy. The purpose is not to reach decisions so much as to share perceptions of classroom management problems and learn of other teachers' attempts to implement positive approaches. One colleague may have adopted a strategy with an individual pupil or the whole class, and some others in the group might agree to try this out on an experimental basis; or the process of group discussion may itself generate an idea which no individual would have been likely to produce in isolation. At a later meeting the implementation of these strategies would then be reviewed.

A peer support group is not a substitute for formal in-service provision: indeed it provides a facility for passing on ideas which individuals have learnt on courses. Nor does it absolve the head of responsibility for discussing problems with individual teachers and giving support. What it does do is to complement formal support provision, enabling teachers to learn from each other and develop skills through discussion and sharing experiences, rather than rely on coping alone or referring pupils to others with more authority or expertise. It is a source of relief to know that you are not alone in having discipline problems, while the collaborative nature of the exercise gives teachers confidence to try out new approaches.

Developing dialogue with parents

Parents are often surprised when they learn about their children's behaviour in school, and teachers sometimes disbelieve parents who say, 'But he/she is no trouble at home'. Yet the evidence shows that children do not necessarily behave the same way at school and home (McGee *et al*. 1984). This is one reason why the Elton Committee urged schools to involve parents at an early stage, before a behaviour problem got out of hand.

Yet teachers are often reluctant to discuss behaviour problems with parents, even though they often hold them responsible. In a study of some London schools, Tizard *et al.* (1988) found that the teachers reported behaviour problems in the case of over a quarter of reception class children and over one-third of top infants, yet only about half the parents had been informed.

Why should this kind of mismatch arise? One reason is the fear that parents might over-react by punishing the child severely. Teachers are also sometimes wary of parents interpreting criticisms of their children as a sign of professional incompetence – which they may be tempted to do if their child behaves reasonably at home. In some cases, teachers want to discuss a problem but the parents will not come into school. Yet behaviour problems will not just go away, and the chances of their amelioration is much higher if parents and teachers work together.

Fortunately, a number of primary schools, including those in inner-city 'deprived' areas, have found ways in which teachers can work constructively with parents over behaviour matters.

(1) *Getting to know parents early in the child's school career*

Making parents feel welcome at the time the child starts school or transfers to junior school helps to pre-empt problems of home-school tension before behaviour problems become serious. Some infant teachers make a point of visiting parents in their homes during the term preceding entry to the reception class. In one study of inner-city schools, it was found that, almost without exception, the teachers are welcomed (Blatchford *et al.* 1982). In some cases, parents of children already in the school have participated with the teachers in this exercise. Whether or not home-visiting is on the agenda, the parents can be invited to visit the school with their children to meet teachers and other parents.

(2) *Involving parents in the curriculum and classroom activities*

The evidence suggests that parents are much more likely to want to be involved in school affairs when they are invited to participate in the child's learning. Home-school projects in reading, writing and mathematics typically attract the majority of parents (see Docking, 1990). Besides benefiting academic achievement, this way of working with parents has positive influences on classroom behaviour. One reason for this is that, because they help to bring parents into school to discuss reading problems, the projects also provide a structure for parents and teachers to get to know each other better. This makes it easier for the teacher to approach the parent, or the parent to approach the teacher, when the child's behaviour is causing concern. Secondly, home-school curriculum projects help parents to establish better relationships with their children as they sit down together for fifteen minutes or so each day to share reading. In setting up a scheme, the school emphasises the importance of making positive comment on the child's progress and of avoiding constant criticism. These have valuable spill-over effects which enhance the child's feelings of worth and competence, which in turn help to improve behaviour. Thirdly, the evidence shows that it is not only children's motivation towards reading that improves, but towards school learning in general (Tizard *et al.* 1982). Partnership with parents through the curriculum can therefore be remarkably fruitful in ways which go beyond formal learning outcomes.

(3) *Positive letters home*

Another constructive strategy is to send positive letters home as a means of reinforcing improved or regularly good behaviour. Parents who get nothing but negative messages about their children will understandably feel hostile to the school and reluctant to cooperate. Positive letters can be linked to the use of charts by which the child and teacher together monitor progress towards specific target behaviours (see p. 52). The Elton Committee recommended that parents receive positive constructive comments about their children's work and behaviour as a matter of course.

(4) *Helping parents to monitor children's behaviour*

Parents can also be more directly involved in monitoring children's in-school behaviour through reward schemes as described in Chapter 5 (see p. 54–5) and the 'success book' idea described in Chapter 6 (see p. 81). Again, this encourages parents, as well as teachers, to reinforce effort and good behaviour rather than concentrate on the problem behaviour.

(5) *Meetings to explore particular issues*

Some schools have found it useful to run discussion groups about behaviour during parents' evenings. An example was given in the last chapter, when parents at one school watched the children dramatise problems of playground behaviour and then discussed the issues with the teachers. In other schools, class teachers have organised discussions with parents about bullying. These sorts of occasions are also important in helping parents to support each other.

Measures such as these should help parents to feel welcome and participating members of the school community, but there may be some who are critical and hostile. Confrontations easily arise if teachers return the hostility. Sometimes the parents' aggressiveness stems from an understandable unwillingness to accept that their child presents behaviour problems; sometimes it reflects weak communication skills, an inability to be assertive without showing anger. Interviews with aggressive parents usually go better if you

- sit by them informally and not on opposite sides of a table which emphasises status
- avoid showing fear, which could reinforce the parent's hostility
- talk slowly and softly
- allow the parents to say what they want to say
- convey to the parents that you recognise the feelings being expressed and understand their difficulties
- don't give the impression that you are blaming the parents but rather that you are trying to see if you can together work out a positive approach.

Lunchtime supervision

Behaviour in the dining room can be a particular problem for schools. Although the head has overall responsibility for midday supervision under the School Teachers' Pay and Conditions regulations, teaching staff are no longer contractually obliged to carry out supervisory duties during the midday break. Teachers may, however, be employed under separate contracts to supervise lunchtime activities, but often the job is done by specially-hired assistants who have no formal training or experience in managing large groups of children. The Elton Report recommended that such training should be provided, but did not suggest just how.

A project in one large Essex primary school set up by Imich and Jefferies (1989) points to some ways in which teaching and non-teaching staff can cooperate to alleviate the problem. Following a support teacher's observations in the dining hall over a period of three weeks, a series of meetings was held with the teaching staff and helpers, the latter coming in their own time. The helpers wanted to discuss ways in which they could control the children effectively. The staff therefore decided to discuss with them positive management strategies. From these discussions, a set of procedures was agreed, and a written record was made for the benefit of newly appointed helpers. Items included:

- admitting to the dining area only children who are behaving satisfactorily;
- not allowing children to leave until everyone at their table has finished and returned the dishes and utensils;
- commending pupils and giving team points for good behaviour;
- informing class teachers about good behaviour so that the pupils concerned received further praise in the classroom;
- reprimanding only when misbehaviour is directly observed and not relying on tale-telling.

The helpers also agreed to wear name-badges so that children could address them properly. Further discussions were held with the helpers each half term.

Secondly, a set of rules and sanctions was drawn up to ensure that helpers managed problem behaviour in a consistent way. For minor misdemeanours, such as pushing, shouting or talking back, offenders had to sit on a chair facing a wall for five minutes in an area away from other children and under an assistant's supervision. For more serious misbehaviour, such as swearing or insolence, the helper gave the offender a yellow card on which was recorded the helper's name, the date and the offence. The child had to obtain the helper's signature for good behaviour each day for a week, and then see the headteacher for signing off. Three yellow cards resulted in parents being contacted and a week's suspension from school during lunchtime. During assembly, these arrangements were carefully explained to the children, who could ask questions and make further suggestions.

The system lead to improved behaviour between pupils and better relationships between pupils and helpers. The helpers felt that they were now better respected, not least because they were operating within a clear framework which the pupils understood and which had the support of the head and staff.

Developing a whole-school policy

The purpose of a whole-school policy is to promote a degree of consensus amongst members of the school community about expected standards of behaviour and how these might be realised and maintained. Ideally, head, class teachers, support teachers, non-teaching staff (e.g. the school secretary, caretaker, lunchtime helpers), pupils, parents, and governors should all be actively involved. Although in reality it may not be feasible for all parties to participate at every stage along the way, the degree of involvement should be such that all affected parties feel the discussions are addressing their main concerns. Because each school will wish to adopt a procedure which best suits its particular circumstances and perceived needs, the suggestions which follow should be regarded as ideas for consideration and not a prescription for every situation.

Since the success of a whole-school policy depends on everyone feeling that their own contribution is important and that the effort is worthwhile, the process demands time. It is important that participants are able to assimilate the range and nature of the problems, and that no one feels rushed into agreements which have not been properly thought through. Fortunately, unlike many other kinds of educational decisions these days, the absence of external deadlines means that a school can set its own timetable. All the same, in order that the initial momentum is not lost, meetings should be reasonably near each other. The whole process usually takes between one and two terms. The policy then needs to be kept under review so that pupils, staff and other members of the school community continue to maintain a sense of ownership.

A member of staff will need to be appointed, or elected, to coordinate the various activities and the organisation of paper work. If the head assumes this responsibility, there is a danger of the policy being thought of as 'his' or 'hers' rather than 'ours'. In a large primary school, the staff may wish to ask two or three of their number to act as a steering group and assist the coordinator.

In the early stages, it is usually best if the head and coordinator do not pre-empt staff discussion by trying to identify all the needs or to lay down a tight schedule of events. Although some structure will be needed, discussion at first should be as open-ended as possible to promote a feeling of involvement. The brainstorming approach is sometimes used, members of the group being invited to make comments and suggestions freely without immediate evaluation from

lack of consultation could undermine consistency

the chair or anybody else. Once everyone feels that they have had their say, it is then appropriate to give the debate some structure by inviting the meeting to categorise the ideas and prioritise them for examination and evaluation.

More structure will be needed to promote the involvement of the pupils. If children are to feel that their views are taken seriously, it is important for teachers not to jump in early with judgemental responses. Equally, it is essential to give regular feedback to explain how the children's comments and suggestions are being used. If there is a Schools Council with a system of class representatives (see next section), the structure for eliciting pupils' perceptions and providing feedback is already in place. The process of pupil participation can be a valuable experience in democratic decision-making for classes at all age levels, and could incorporate the design and analysis of questionnaires and surveys about particular issues such as playground behaviour and facilities for play, bullying and harassment, problems encountered by dinner helpers, and the structure of the school day.

Parents are probably the most difficult constituency to involve in policy-making. They are not, as a body, on site as a matter of course, and they may not respond to invitations. Teachers might be understandably cautious about the possibility of having to deal with parents whose 'involvement' consists of blaming the school for poor discipline – the 'Now when I was at school no pupil would ever dare . . . ' kind of comment. It is probably more manageable to work with groups of parents in developing policies for areas of concern such as playground behaviour and bullying to which parents can relate more easily (see p. 94). Unlike classroom conduct, these are matters which have a more obvious bearing on children's out-of-school behaviour and for which the opportunity for parents and teachers to share perceptions and approaches would seem particularly fitting and likely to be helpful to both parties.

Parents may be more ready to participate if the invitation comes personally from their child's class teacher. A class meeting also allows the teacher and parents to get to know each other better and for parents to learn from each other. There can be a sharing of perceptions about what counts as good and bad behaviour, about problems of managing children at home and school, and about appropriate sanctions. One technique is to start off with a simple open-ended questionnaire which could be completed individually or in sub-groups. For example, parents in twos or threes could be invited to write down examples of what they consider to be good and bad behaviour in the classroom, in the playground, in travelling to and from school, and at home. These could then be discussed, the objective being to see what degree of consensus exists about expected standards of behaviour.

The list in the box on page 116 shows a range of matters which might be included in a whole-school policy. It is important, however, that the actual agenda is drawn up by the school, which will want to focus on those issues which are particulary relevant to its situation.

A case study

We now examine the way one urban primary school went about making its whole-school behaviour policy. The case study is presented as an illustration of a procedure that one school found useful in its particular circumstances with all the teaching staff, dinner helpers and children participating.

The school, St. Anne's in Kennington, London, is a Roman Catholic foundation with about 280 children aged 4 to 11. There is a wide variety of ethnic backgrounds and twenty-one first-languages. Apart from the head, the staff comprises twelve full-time and two part-time teachers, plus helpers and a nursery nurse. The children are mainly from families of very low incomes, and about one-third of the children have free school meals. Teaching accommodation is split between the original three-storey Victorian school and two buildings erected in the 1920s. Although imaginative use has been made of the space available, the configuration of rooms, levels, halls, cloakrooms, stairways, toilets, corridors and entrances appears to conform to no rational criteria, creates severe problems of movement and communication, and does little to foster a sense of community. The site is surrounded by busy main roads, play facilities are restricted, and there are no green areas.

The appointment of a new head and several new teachers created the opportunity to respond to the staff's felt need to think afresh about policies and practices for managing pupil behaviour. One teacher agreed to accept the role of coordinator as part of her job description for one year, which also included attendance at INSET courses to up-date her knowledge of behaviour management. When the staff first met to implement the project, discussion ranged widely. Teachers wanted to share their perceptions of the causes of behaviour problems, of critical times of the day and areas in the school, of examples of successful and of unsuccessful classroom management practices, school rules, rewards and punishments.

SOME POSSIBLE TOPICS FOR INCLUSION IN A WHOLE-SCHOOL BEHAVIOUR POLICY

Teaching and classroom management styles

School rules – how they should be decided, and how communicated to pupils and parents

Behaviour during playtimes and lunchtime, including lunch and playground supervision, wet playtimes, playground facilities and equipment, problems raised by football and other games, arrangements for entering the school buildings, tuck shop, lunchtime activities

Reward systems

Punishments and policy for referrals to the head

Policies to deal with bullying and harassment

Support for class teachers when children present special behavioural needs, including policy and procedure for involving support agencies

Liaison with parents about behaviour problems and good behaviour

The use and impact of the physical environment on behaviour and feelings of 'belonging', e.g. classroom layout, display areas, corridors, stairways, toilets, play areas

How children are grouped

School uniform

Regulations about what children are allowed to wear and bring to school, e.g. jewellery, toys, sweets

The contribution of the curriculum in generating feelings of self-worth and mutual respect. This includes discussion of cross-curricular issues such as race and equal opportunities for boys and girls, and of curriculum organisation such as the desirability of organising a special programme of activities in personal and social education

Opportunities for children to succeed in non-academic as well as academic pursuits, including school clubs and other extra-curricular activities

The structure of the school day, e.g. bell times, lengths and positioning of lunch and playtimes

Use of support staff, parents and other adults in the school and classroom

Strategies for monitoring behaviour standards

Since there seemed to be so many issues which needed to be addressed, the staff broke into groups of threes and fours to examine the problems, some of which were common between groups. On re-assembling to pool ideas, it emerged that there was general agreement about many matters. Some factors influencing behaviour were recognised to be beyond the school's control, for example home circumstances, the layout of the school, staff changes, and wet weather at playtime! Other factors, however, were regarded as within the school's control. These included inconsistency of teaching styles and management practices, arrangements for playtimes and lunchtimes (regarded as the most difficult times of the day to manage), the nature and enforcement of school rules, and the manner in which teachers responded to behaviour problems. The discussion also produced lengthy lists of management practices judged to be most and least effective.

The coordinator produced a document reflecting the general consensus of this meeting, and used this as a basis for further discussion when the staff met again about a fortnight later. There was little difficulty in agreeing to give new emphasis to all the positive strategies which staff had identified. These included: praising children for good behaviour as well as for work: making a point of getting to know children better and encouraging them: pre-empting behaviour problems by taking care over lesson planning and classroom organisation; trying hard to be consistent and fair in the use of sanctions: apologising when a misunderstanding arose; and endeavouring to maintain a sense of humour. Further 'needs' were also identified, such as for teachers to have clear rules governing behaviour in the classroom, for certain school rules to be clarified (e.g. about wearing PE kit, bringing jewellery to school, and allowing children to go to the toilet during lesson time), and for teachers to distinguish between minor and major incidents when responding to misbehaviour.

It was then decided to focus on the problems of school rules and behaviour out of lesson time. Teachers expressed concern about rough behaviour and a spate of injuries in the playground, commenting that contributory factors could be the limited space and inadequate facilities for play, together with difficulties of supervising so many children. Staff also felt that there were too many school rules and too many negative and unrealistic ones. A clear procedure for dealing with misbehaviour was also needed to protect the dinner helpers and promote consistency amongst all staff, several of whom had only recently joined the school.

At this point it was considered essential that the staff should listen to what the pupils had to say. As a way forward, it was decided that teachers would ask the children in their classes to complete a questionnaire (verbally in the case of infant classes) and discuss the responses. One group of questions tapped the children's awareness of existing rules and sanctions, since it was thought that a general lack of understanding would suggest problems of communication and presentation. In the event the children appeared quite knowledgeable. Another group invited suggestions about rules that were needed, particularly in the playground, and also asked for ideas concerning suitable rewards and sanctions. To find out whether a greater range of opportunities should be provided for play and lunchtimes, the children were also asked to make suggestions for school clubs, playground equipment, and games. Lastly, the children were asked to say whether they played mostly with others in their class or another class, and, if the latter, whether this was in their own year. This information would be used to inform any decision which might be made to pair classes for staggered playtimes.

Further staff meetings were then arranged to discuss the children's responses, and a draft set of new rules and practices were drawn up as a result. Each proposal was then discussed with the pupils in class, or subjected to a pupil poll, and the dinner ladies were also brought into the discussion before the policy was finalised. The process had taken the best part of two terms to complete, and the school is now experimenting with the new arrangements. These are:

(1) STAGGERED PLAYTIMES
These reduce supervision and congestion problems. Although some teachers saw social benefits in pairing classes from different years, it was decided for the time being to pair within years since the great majority of children had said that they preferred to play with their own age group.

(2) FACILITIES FOR MORE CONSTRUCTIVE PLAY
The children now have access to a variety of equipment such as skipping ropes, hoops, bean bags, marbles, big toys for the reception class, and boxes of indoor activities for wet weather. One playground

area is set aside for football, and classes use it in rotation. The staff also try to encourage non-competitive games.

(3) INDOOR LUNCHTIME ACTIVITIES

These are provided for those who do not wish to play outside. They include a prayer group, story reading, facilities for listening to taped stories, and a range of clubs (e.g. art, drama, chess, dancing, model-making)

(4) CERTIFICATES FOR GOOD BEHAVIOUR

Teachers in both the classroom and playground, together with lunchtime helpers, have agreed to look for and acknowledge instances of pro-social conduct, particularly among children whose good behaviour does not easily get noticed. The children are thanked or praised, as appropriate, and entries made in 'good behaviour books' (with cheerfully decorated covers bearing bright smiley faces). Examples of items recorded are: 'Looking after Paula when she fell over', 'Giving a hoop back nicely to an infant', 'Fetching a coat for the duty teacher on her own initiative', 'Volunteering to search round the school when some PE equipment was missing', and (for three children) 'Giving up five playtimes to tidy the classroom'. Children whose names appear three times in a single week are awarded a special certificate by the head teacher in assembly and encouraged to show this to their parents. It was also agreed to keep parallel records of unacceptable behaviour and to liaise with parents if three incidents occurred in any one week.

(5) A NEW SET OF SCHOOL RULES

A number of useful suggestions had been made in the questionnaire responses, and it was decided to conduct a school poll on each of these. The staff then agreed a new set of rules which took account of the children's ideas. The items included some which drew attention to general principles, for example 'We will be polite and kind to everybody in the school', while others specified particular desired behaviours, for example 'We will be as quiet as possible on school corridors and pick up coats or bags on the floor'. Two models were produced, one in which all the rules were positively phrased and the other in which there was a mixture of positive and negative wording. Eventually it was decided to use the latter format for the time being.

Although the staff realised that this was not 'according to Elton', it was felt that the absence of any 'We won'ts' would be too much of a change from the previous system. Some rules, such as those prohibiting jewellery or banning football before school, were also difficult to word positively. However, most of the negative rules were paired with a positive one, for example 'We will stay in our own playground' and 'We won't climb in the playground'.

The staff agreed a statement to preface the rules and set out guiding principles:

> The rules developed and agreed by staff and pupils at this school are based on the understanding that we will be considerate and kind to each other at all times and work and play safely together
> We will respect the ways in which each one is different and enjoy and value the special contribution of each one. We will tell someone else as soon as we can if something is worrying us. We will listen to those who look after us, especially our teachers and helpers, and try to do what they ask straight away.

(6) COMMUNICATION OF RULES

The children were each given a copy of the rules which they were asked to sign and show to their parents. They were also asked to design a poster depicting up to four rules. This encouraged parents and children to talk about the new policy since the children undertook the activity at home. A competition was organised, and the selected posters were displayed in classrooms and at key points around the school.

(7) CONTRACTS

For those experiencing special behaviour difficulties, teachers are experimenting with contracts to help the children achieve realistic target behaviours, monitor their own progress, and receive reinforcement for improved behaviour. An example was given in Chapter 4 (figure 4.1).

For those experiencing special behaviour difficulties, teachers are experimenting with contracts to help the children achieve realistic target behaviours, monitor their own progress, and receive reinforcement for improved behaviour.

At the beginning of the week, the teacher and child agree on a specific objective, which the child records at the top of a contract document and signs. An example would be 'I will try to stay in my seat and raise my hand if I want to move'. During the day, the teacher uses praise to reinforce the child's attempts to honour the contract. If at any time the child feels it necessary to break the contract, he or she records a reason. At the end of each day, the child and teacher discuss progress and both enter a comment on the contract sheet. The child is thus provided with a structured framework which makes the achievement of more acceptable behaviour a manageable proposition and encourages the teacher and child to improve their relationship through constructive dialogue.

The development of the policy at this school did not directly involve parents. However, the head teacher was able to elicit parental concerns and viewpoints during the course of interviews which she was conducting at the school as part of her MA research. Additionally, all parents were kept informed about the policy at various points during its development, and their support was enlisted through the poster competition. Also, the certificates for good behaviour are taken home, and there is now a structure for systematic liaison with parents over behaviour problems.

At the time of writing, the new arrangements are in their infancy and have not yet been formally reviewed. However, the head and coordinator report that behaviour has noticeably improved, particularly in the playground. The staff believe that the high profile given to the development of a new policy and the active involvement of all the children at various stages, has in itself helped to raise levels of awareness and improve standards of conduct. The dinner helpers, who were consulted along the line, seem much happier now, though they need encouragement to look for and systematically record incidents of good behaviour. Typically, three or four certificates for good behaviour are presented in assembly each Monday morning, while the need to contact parents for incidents of unacceptable behaviour has been negligible. The 'good behaviour' books have proved an incentive not only for children to act more considerately but also to prompt staff to look out for thoughtful and polite behaviour. The entries in the books also help to monitor the success of the new policy.

School councils

School councils offer a permanent structure by which pupils are involved in decision-making. Although they are often a feature of 'progressive' and secondary schools, councils in primary schools are comparatively rare. Yet involving pupils in democratic decision-making has an important contribution to make to children's affective and social development and their understanding of group management problems. It is, of course, important that the children are encouraged to listen to each other and to argue their case in an unthreatening atmosphere.

Richard Brading (1989) has evaluated the working and achievements of school councils in four inner-London primary schools. These meet fortnightly or monthly and comprise one boy and one girl from each class, elected for a fixed period. Although council meetings are chaired by the headteacher, class meetings chaired by one of the pupil representatives are held before council meetings to elicit suggestions and report back. In this way *all* pupils are involved. Certain constraints are imposed upon the councils' powers: for instance, the head's intervention is required for major matters of policy, and children are not allowed to make negative comments about named individuals. Nonetheless, the matters debated are real issues which materially affect the children's lives and relate to their personal problems. Items included in agendas have included name-calling, bullying, lining up, playground equipment and games, and wet play arrangements. For instance, the council of one school was instrumental in securing designated playground areas to prevent those playing football dominating all the space, while the council in another school faced the same problem by declaring Wednesday a 'no football' day. An anti-bullying policy was drawn up in one of the schools. This outlawed specific practices such as hitting or kicking people, name-calling and swearing, laid down the procedure to be taken by victims and measures to deal with the children who bullied. In a series of interviews, the children claimed that the playgrounds were now safer places and that there was a nicer atmosphere in school.

As might be expected, Brading found that each school had faced problems in running council meetings fairly, and some decisions had proved unpopular or unworkable. Such experiences are, of course, an important part of the children's social education and training in democratic procedures. From the responses to a questionnaire, it was clear that, overall, pupils at each school valued the opportunity to express their feelings and bring about change. As one child said, 'I think it's a good idea to have a school council because it makes the school a happier place to be in'.

At Hillbrook Primary School in Tooting, where Brading is currently acting head, a school council has been introduced with two particularly interesting features. One is the involvement of infants.

since these children are considered too young to play a direct part in the council meetings, they are represented by top junior children, who visit the infant clasrooms to gather suggestions and report back from council meetings. The other innovation involves a rota whereby each class and its teacher in turn observe the council meetings. This enables the children to understand a little about how democratically elected bodies conduct business and deal with procedural problems. The observers also benefit from watching the representatives listening to each other and resolving dilemmas when different interests are at stake.

The term 'partnership' in education is typically used to describe a collaborative approach involving teachers and parents. Some of the projects described in this chapter and earlier ones demonstrate ways in which pupils, as well as parents, can be successfully involved as partners. Such a way of working emphasises the interdependence of each member of the school community, and how the behaviour of any one party affects, and is affected by, the others. Partnership practices are an attempt to promote a community spirit, a deeper and more mutual understanding of the issues, and a greater sense of commitment to school policies than is otherwise normally experienced. As more primary schools develop collaborative working styles, they should find the experience rewarding socially, educationally and managerially.

Further Reading

Classroom Management Issues

Bull, S. L. and Solity, J. E. (1987) *Classroom Management: Principles to Practice*. Beckenham: Croom Helm.

Cohen, L. and Manion, L. (1989) *A Guide to Teaching Practice* (3rd edition). London: Routledge.

Docking, J. W. (1987) *Control and Discipline in Schools: Perspecitves and Aproaches* (2nd edition). London: Paul Chapman Publishing.

Gray, J. and Richer, J. (1988) *Classroom Responses to Disruptive Behaviour*. London: Macmillan Education.

Merrett, F. and Wheldall, K. (1990) *Positive Teaching in the Primary School*. London: Paul Chapman Publishing.

Montgomery, D. (1989) *Managing Behaviour Problems*. Sevenoaks: Hodder and Stoughton.

Encouraging Positive Thinking

Docking, J. W. (ed) (1990) *Education and Alienation in the Junior School*. Basingstoke: Falmer Press.

Resources:

Canfield, J. and Wells, H. C. (1976) *100 Ways to Enhance Self-concept in the Classroom*. Englewood Cliffs, N. J.: Prentice-Hall.

Leech, N. and Wooster, A. D. (1986) *Personal and Social Skills*. Exeter: Religious and Moral Education Press.

Masheder, M. (1986) *Let's Cooperate*. London: Peace Education Project. (Further materials are obtainable from the PEP, Dick Shepherd House, 6 Endsleigh St., London, WC1H 0DX.)

Nicholas, F. M. (1987) *Coping with Conflict*. Wisbech, Cambs.: Learning Development Aids.

Smith, C. (1983) *Promoting the Social development of Young Children: Strategies and Activities*. Palo Alto, CA: Mayfield Publishing.

Playground Behaviour and Bullying

See the following in the references lists: Besag (1989), Blatchford (1989), Roland and Munthe (1989), Tattum and Lane (1989).

The following booklet, obtainable from the Faculty of Education, South Glamorgan Institute of Higher Education, Cyncoed Cardiff, CF2 6XD, contains suggestions and includes a list of resource materials and further reading: Tattum, D. and Herbert, G. (1990) *Bullying: a Positive Response: Advice for Parents, Governors and Staff in Schools.*

Kidscape, 82 Brook Street, London W1Y 1YG, produces suggestions for teachers.

Parental Involvement

Atkin, J., Bastiani, J. and Goode, J. (1988) *Listening to Parents.* Beckenham: Croom Helm.
Docking, J. W. (1990) *Primary Schools and Parents: Rights, Responsibilities and Relationships.* Sevenoaks: Hodder and Stoughton.

Whole-School Policies

Watkins, C. and Wagner, P. (1987) *School Discipline: A Whole-School Approach.* Oxford: Basil Blackwell.

References

Aronfreed, J. (1976) 'Moral development from the standpoint of a general psychological theory', in Lickona, T. (ed) *Moral Development and Behaviour*. New York: Holt, Rinehart & Winston.

Barker, G. P. and Graham, S. (1987) 'Developmental study of praise and blame as attributional cues', *Journal of Educational Psychology*, 79, 62–66.

Bar-Tal, D. (1984) 'The effects of teachers' behaviour on pupils' attributions: a review', in Barnes, P., Oates, J., Chaman, J., Lee, V. and Czerniewska, P. (eds) *Personality, Development and Learning*. Sevenoaks: Hodder and Stoughton.

Belilios, E. M. (1990) *Playground Behaviour in a Pre-Preparatory Boys' School: A Case Study with Specific Reference to the Emerging Attitudes of Bullies and Victims*. BEd Case Study, Roehampton Institute of Higher Education.

Bennett, N. and Cass, A. (1988) 'The effects of group composition on group interactive processes and pupil understanding', *British Educational Research Journal*, 15, 19–32

Bennett, N., Desforges, C., Cockburn, A. and Wilkinson, B. (1984) *The Quality of Pupil Learning Experiences*. Hillsdale, N. J.: Erlbaum

Besag, V. (1989) *Bullies and Victims in Schools*. Milton Keynes: Open University Press.

Blatchford, P. (1989) *Playtime in the Primary School: Problems and Improvements*. Windsor: NFER-Nelson.

Blatchford, P., Battle, S. and Mays, J. (1982) *The First Transition: Home to Pre-School*. Windsor: NFER-Nelson.

Blatchford, P., Burke, J., Farquhar, C., Plewis, I. and Tizard, B. (1987) 'A systematic observation study of children's behaviour at infant school', *Research Papers in Education*, 2, 47–61.

Boggiano, A. K. and Ruble, D. N. (1979) 'Competence and the overjustification effect: a developmental study', *Journal of Personality and Social Psychology*, 37, 1462–1468.

Boggiano, A. K., Ruble, D. N. and Pittman, T. S. (1982) 'The mastery hypothesis and the overjustification effect', *Social Cognition*, 1, 38–49.

Brading, R. (1989) *School Councils in Primary Schools*. MA Dissertation, Roehampton Institute of Higher Education.

Brattesani, K., Weinstein, R. S. and Marshall, H. H. (1984), 'Student perceptions of differential teacher treatment as moderators of teacher expectation effects', *Journal of Educational Psychology*, 76, 236–247.

Brophy, J. (1981) 'Teacher praise: a functional analysis', *Review of Educational Research*, 15, 5–32.

Brophy, J. (1983) 'Research on the self-fulfilling prophecy and teacher expectations', *Journal of Educational Psychology*, 75, 631–661.

Burden, M., Emsley, M. and Constable, H. (1988) 'Encouraging progress in collaborative group-work', *Education 3–13*, 16, 51–56.

Cheeseman, P. L. and Watts, P. E. (1985) *Positive Behaviour Management: a Manual for Teachers*. London: Croom Helm.

Croll, P. and Moses, D. (1985) *One in Five*. London: Routledge & Kegan Paul.

Condry, J. and Chambers, J. (1979) 'Intrinsic motivation and the process of learning', in Lepper, M. D. and Greene, D. (eds) *The Hidden Costs of Reward*. Hillsdale, N. J.: Erlbaum.

Cooper, H. M. and Tom, D. Y. H. (1984) 'Teacher expectation research: a review with implications for classroom instruction', *Elementary School Journal*, 85, 77–89.

Coopersmith, J. (1967) *The Antecedents of Self-esteem*. San Francisco: W. H. Freeman.

Coulby, J. and Coulby, D. (1990) 'Intervening in junior classrooms', in Docking, J. W. (ed) *Alienation in the Junior School*. Basingstoke: Falmer Press.

Coxhead, P. and Gupta, R. M. (1989) 'A survey of educational psychologists' views on the delivery of behaviour modification', *Educational Studies*, 15, 15–22.

Cullingford, C. (1988) 'School rules and children's attitude to discipline', *Educational Research*, 30, 3–8.

Daux, T. (1988) 'Fostering self-discipline in schools', *Primary Teaching Studies*, 4, 66–73.

Davies, B. (1979) 'Children's perceptions of social interaction in school', *CORE*, 3, Fiche 11F9.

Dawson, R. (1987) 'What concerns teachers about their pupils?', in Hastings, N. and Schwieso, J. (eds) *New Directions in Educational Psychology: 2 – Behaviour and Motivation in the Classroom*. Lewes: Falmer Press.

Department of Education and Science (1989) *Discipline in Schools: Report of the Committee of Enquiry chaired by Lord Elton*. London: HMSO.

Docking, J. W. (1990) *Primary Schools and Parents: Rights, Responsibilities and Relationships*. Sevenoaks: Hodder and Stoughton.

Doyle, W. and Carter, K. (1986) 'Academic tasks in classrooms', in Hammersely, A. (ed) *Case Studies in Classroom Research*. Milton Keynes: Open University Press.

Dweck, C. S. (1985) 'Intrinsic motivation, perceived control and self-evaluation maintenance: an achievement goal analysis', in Ames, C. and Ames, R. (eds) *Research on Motivation in Education. Volume 2: The Classroom Milieu*. London: Academic Press.

Fincham, F. D. (1983) 'Developmental dimensions in attribution theory', in Jaspers, J., Fincham, F. D. and Hewstone, M. (eds) *Attribution Theory and Research*. London: Academic Press.

Fry, P. S. (1987) 'Classroom environments and their effect on problem and non-problem children's classroom behaviour and motivation' in Hastings, N. and Schwieso, J. (eds) *New Directions in Educational Psychology: 2 – Behaviour and Motivation in the Classroom*. Lewes: Falmer Press.

Galton, M., Simon, B. and Croll, P. (1980) *Inside the Primary School Classroom*. London: Routledge & Kegan Paul.

Gurney, P. (1990) 'The enhancement of self-esteem in junior classrooms', in Docking, J. W. (ed) *Alienation in the Junior School*. Basingstoke: Falmer Press.

Her Majesty's Inspectorate for Schools (1987) *Good Behaviour and Discipline in Schools* (Education Observed 5). London: Department of Education and Science.

Hoffman, M. L. (1970) Conscience, personality and socialization techniques', *Human Development*, 13, 90–126.

Imich, A. and Jeffries, K. (1989) 'The management of lunchtime behaviour', *Support for Learning*, 4, 46–52.

Johnson, D. W. and Johnson, R. T. (1982) 'Having your cake and eating it too: maximising achievement, cognitive-social development and socialisation through cooperative learning'. Paper presented to the American Pychological Association Convention, Washington DC.

Kagan, J., Mussen, P. H. and Conger, J. J. (1967) *Child Development and Personality*. London: Harper & Row.

Kanouse, D. E., Gumpert, P. and Canavan-Gumpert, D. (1981) 'The semantics of praise', in Harvey, J. H., Ickes, W. and Kidds, R. F. (eds) *New Directions in Attribution Research*, Vol. 3. Hillsdale, N. J.: Erlbaum.

Kohlberg, L. (1968) 'The child as moral philosopher', *Psychology Today*, 2, 25–30.

Kounin, J. (1970) *Discipline and Group Management in Classrooms*. New York: Holt, Rinehart & Winston.

Laslett, R. (1982) 'A children's court for bullies', *Special Education, Forward Trends*, 9, 9–11.

Leech, N. and Wooster, A. D. (1986) *Personal and Social Skills*. Exeter: Religious and Moral Education Press.

Lepper, M. R. and Green, D. (eds.) (1978) *The Hidden Costs of Rewards*. Hillsdale, N. J.: Erlbaum.

Lerner, M. (1970) 'The desire for justice and reaction to victims', in Macaulay, J. and Berkowitz, L. (eds) *Altruism and Helping Behaviour*. New York: Academic Press.

Light, P. (1979) *The Development of Social Sensitivity*. Cambridge: Cambridge University Press.

Little, A. W. (1985) 'The child's understanding of the causes of academic success and failure: a case study of British schoolchildren', *British Journal of Educational Psychology*, 55, 11–23.

McGee, R., Sylva, P. A. and Williams, S. (1984) 'Behaviour problems in a population of seven-year-old children', *Journal of Child Psychiatry and Psychology*, 25, 251–259.

Merrett, F. E. (1985) *Encouragement Works Better than Punishment*. Birmingham: Positive Products.

Merrett, F. E. and Wheldall, K. (1986) 'Natural rates of teacher approval and disapproval in British primary and middle school classrooms', *British Journal of Educational Psychology*, 57, 95–103.

Mitman, A. L. and Lash, A. A. (1988) 'Students' perceptions of their academic standing and classroom behaviour', *The Elementary School Journal*, 89, 55–68.

Mortimore, P., Sammons, P., Stoll, L., Lewis, D., and Ecob, R. (1988) *School Matters: the junior years*. Wells: Open Books.

Neill, S. R. St J. (1989) 'The effects of facial expression and posture on children's reported responses to teacher nonverbal communication', *British Educational Research Journal*, 15, 195–204.

Newson, J. and Newson, E. (1984) 'Parents' perspectives on children's behaviour in school', in Frude, N. and Gault, G. (eds) *Disruptive Behaviour in Schools*. Chichester: John Wiley.

Nicholls, J. G. (1983) 'Conceptions of ability and achievement motivation: a theory and its implications for education', in Paris, S. G., Olson, G. M. and Stevenson, H. W. (eds) *Learning and Motivation in the Classroom*. Hillsdale, N. J.: Erlbaum.

O'Leary, K. D. and O'Leary, S. E. (1977) *Classroom Management*. New York: Pergamon Press.

Olweus, D. (1978) *Aggression in Schools: Bullies and Whipping Boys*. Washington DC: Hemisphere.

Piaget, J. (1932) *The Moral Judgement of the Child*. London: Routledge & Kegan Paul.

Pollard, A. and Tann, S. (1988) *Reflective Teaching in the Primary School*. London: Cassell.

Purcheon, V. (1990) 'A touchy subject', *Times Educational Supplement*, 11 May.

Purkey, W. W. (1970) *Self-concept and School Achievement*. New York: Prentice Hall.

Rogers. C. (1987) 'Attribution theory and motivation in school', in Hastings, N. and Schwieso, J. (eds) *New Directions in Educational Psychology: 2 – Behaviour and Motivation in the Classroom*. Lewes: Falmer Press.

Rogers, C. (1990) 'Disaffection in the junior years: a perspective from theories of motivation', in Docking, J. W. (ed) *Alienation in the Junior School*. Basingstoke: Falmer Press.

Rohrkemper, M. and Brophy, J. E. (1983) 'Teachers' thinking about problem students', in Levine, J. M. and Wang, M. C. (eds) *Teacher and Student Perceptions: Implications for Learning*. Hillsdale, N. J.: Erlbaum.

Roland, E. and Munthe, E. (1989) *Bullying: An International Perspective*. London: David Fulton Publishers.

Roland, E. (1989) 'Bullying: the Scandinavian research tradition', in Roland, E. and Munthe, E. (eds) *Bullying: An International Perspective*. London: David Fulton Publishers.

Rosenfield, P., Lambert, N. M. and Black, A. (1985) 'Desk arrangement effects on pupil classroom behaviour', *Journal of Educational Psychology*, 77, 101–108.

Rosenthal, R. and Jacobson, L. (1968) *Pygmalion in the Classroom*. New York: Holt, Rinehart & Winston.

Saunders, L. (1989) 'A behaviour modification programme to increase desirable but infrequent behaviour in a 7-year-old boy', *Links*, 14, 20–26.

School Examinations and Assessment Council (1990) *A Guide to Teacher Assessment*. London: Heinemann.

Schunk, D.H. (1987) 'Self-efficacy and motivated learning', in Hastings, N. and Schwieso, J. (eds) *New Directions in Educational Psychology: 2 – Behaviour and Motivation in the Classroom*. Lewes: Falmer Press.

Stephenson, P. and Smith, D. (1989) 'Bullying in the junior school', in Tattum, D. and Lane, D. (eds) *Bullying in Schools*. Stoke-on-Trent: Trentham Books.

Tattum, D. (1989) 'Violence and aggression in schools', in Tattum, D. and Lane, D. (eds) (1989) *Bullying in Schools*. Stoke-on-Trent: Trentham Books.

Tattum, D. and Herbert, G. (1990) *Bullying: A Positive Response*. Cardiff: South Glamorgan Institute of Higher Education.

Tattum, D. and Lane, D. (eds) (1989) *Bullying in Schools*. Stoke-on-Trent: Trentham Books.

Tizard, B., Blatchford, P., Burke, J., Farquhar, C. and Plewis, I. (1988) *Young Children at School in the Inner City*. Hove: Erlbaum.

Tizard, B., Schofield, W.N. and Hewison, J. (1982) 'Collaboration between teachers and parents in assisting children's reading', *British Journal of Educational Psychology*, 52, 1–15.

Weiner, B. (1979) 'A theory of motivation for some classroom experiences', *Journal of Educational Psychology*, 71, 3–25.

West, C. and Wheldall, K. (1989) 'Waiting for teacher: the frequency and duration of times children spend waiting for teacher attention in infant school classrooms', *British Education Research Journal*, 15, 205–216.

Wheldall, K., Bevan, K. and Shortall, K. (1986) 'A touch of reinforcement: the effects of contingent touch on the classroom behaviour of young children', *Educational Review*, 38, 207–216.

Wheldall, K. and Glynn, T. (1989) *Effective Classroom Teaching*. Oxford: Basil Blackwell.

Wheldall, K. and Merrett, F. (1988) 'What classroom behaviours do primary school teachers say they find most troublesome?', *Educational Review*, 40, 13–28.

White, P. (1988) 'The playground project: a democratic learning experience', in Lauder, H. and Brown, P. (eds) *Education in Search of a Future*. Basingstoke: Falmer Press.

Index